Art Therapy and Learning Disabilities

"Don't guess my happiness!"

Edited by
Stephanie Bull and
Kevin O'Farrell

Routledge
Taylor & Francis Group

LONDON AND NEW YORK

First published 2012 by Routledge
27 Church Road, Hove, East Sussex, BN3 2FA

Simultaneously published in the USA and Canada
by Routledge
711 Third Avenue, New York NY 10017

Routledge is an imprint of the Taylor & Francis Group, an informa business

British Library Cataloguing in Publication Data
A catalogue record for this book is available from the British Library

Library of Congress Cataloging in Publication Data
    Art therapy and learning disabilities: don't guess my happiness! / edited
by Stephanie Bull and Kevin O'Farrell.
        p. cm.
    Includes bibliographical references and index.
    ISBN 978-0-415-58323-7 (hardback) — ISBN 978-0-415-58324-4 (pbk.)
    1. Learning disabled—Rehabilitation. 2. Art therapy. I. Bull, Stephanie.
    II. O'Farrell, Kevin, 1969–
    RC394.L37A78 2012
    616.89'1656—dc23   2011039485

ISBN: 978-0-415-58323-7 (hbk)
ISBN: 978-0-415-58324-4 (pbk)

Typeset in Times New Roman by Keystroke, Station Road, Codsall, Wolverhampton

Contents

Illustrations

Figures

Plates

Between pages 108–109

Contributors

Elizabeth Ashby has been working as an art therapist with people who have learning disabilities for thirteen years. She is employed by an NHS trust in the Midlands, and is engaged in research for a Ph.D. connected with her work. Liz is also active in the British Association of Art Therapists (BAAT) Art Therapy and Learning Disability Special Interest Group (ATLD SIG) and is part of a group developing guidelines for art therapists working with people who have learning disabilities.

Quentin Bruckland graduated from Brunel University in 1996 with a BA (Hons) in Textiles and Surface Decoration. After that Quentin worked for a number of textile studios and design houses and successfully sold his designs in the Japanese, Italian and Australian markets. In 2000, he started his studies for his MA in Art Therapy at Hertfordshire University. He has held the position of Senior Art Therapist at the Epilepsy Society since 2003. He works with individuals who live with epilepsy, learning disabilities and complex needs in residential care on site within the Epilepsy Society. He also works for the National Hospital for Neurology and Neurosurgery within the Sir William Gower's Assessment and Diagnostic Unit for the treatment and diagnosis of seizure activity, running art therapy sessions on an in-patient basis.

Stephanie Bull graduated from West Surrey College of Art and Design with a BA (Hons) in Ceramics. She went on to train as an art therapist at St Albans School of Art (University of Hertfordshire), qualifying in 1993. Since then, she has worked as an art therapist with people who have learning disabilities for more than fifteen years. She has supervised MA students on placement and has been a guest lecturer at Roehampton University.

Jane Caven trained in St Albans and qualified as an art therapist in 1991. Since then she has worked for the East London NHS Foundation Trust, in adult mental health services (1991– 1998) and within a specialist community learning disabilities team (1998– present). Jane works with a wide range of people with learning disabilities, including those with autism, those with profound learning disabilities and complex needs, and those with mental health difficulties. She offers both individual and group work. Jane has run groups for people with autism, women, and in partnership with a project that supports young people with learning disabilities in transition (from school). In 2005, Jane completed a Masters in Research in Art Psychotherapy at Goldsmiths, where she researched the use of iconic characters and stories from popular culture in art therapy sessions with people with learning disabilities. Jane is an approved British Association of Art Therapist Private Practitioner.

Kim Dee trained in art therapy at St Albans School of Art (University of Hertfordshire), qualifying in 1994. She has worked with people with learning disabilities for over twenty years, much of that time based in the East End of London. She has also worked in acute mental health services and learning disability services and is currently a member of the Community Learning Disability Service in Tower Hamlets. Kim has provided training on art therapy and learning disabilities as a guest lecturer at Goldsmiths University and BAAT Foundation courses. Kim is a member of BAAT's Learning Disability Special Interest Group. She is particularly interested in the use of multimedia in therapy including film, animation and photography. In addition to her art therapy work, Kim has led projects which include supporting a group of people with learning disabilities in Tower Hamlets to film, produce and publish a DVD and training pack on how to complain about services, called 'Would You Complain?' She has also facilitated health staff in supporting people with learning disabilities to make multimedia health action plans.

Sandra Goody trained as a sculptor and for six years worked on various art projects with adults who experienced mental health difficulties. In 2000, she qualified as an art psychotherapist after studying at the Northern programme in Sheffield. Since then she has been working in LDCAMHS – venturing at times into adult and forensic services all within the Tees, Esk and Wear NHS Valleys Trust. For the past two years, Sandra has co-ordinated the BAAT Art Therapy Learning Disability Special Interest Group, a focus of which has been the development of a guidelines document aimed at supporting practitioners working with people who have learning disabilities.

Kevin O'Farrell gained a degree in history and sociology in 1992 and went on to qualify as an art therapist at the University of Hertfordshire in 1999. He has worked in the NHS for over ten years, within the Hampshire area. Prior to this he worked for social services within a learning disability residential setting for four years. He is a Health Professions Council Registered Art Therapist and a member of BAAT.

Emma Shallcross studied fine art and sculpture at The Manchester Metropolitan University, graduating in 2000 with a Bachelor of Arts degree. She qualified with an MA in Art Psychotherapy at Goldsmiths-University of London in 2006. Emma has worked in a variety of clinical and non-clinical settings within the area of special needs and learning disabilities. In 2007, she set up an art therapy service within a social service setting for a safe house for women with learning disabilities who had suffered abuse, and presented a talk for the E1 London regional group (BAAT) titled 'Saying Goodbye', raising issues for people with learning disabilities whose key workers or staff leave. Currently, Emma supports adults with hearing impairment and learning disabilities or mental health issues (not art therapy).

Sandra Storey gained a degree in fine art in 1983 and went on to qualify as an art therapist at Sheffield University in 1985. She is a Health Professions Council Registered Art Therapist who has worked in the health service for over twenty-five years. She worked initially in adult mental health and then in child, adolescent and family and adult learning disability teams. Sandra has focused on her work in learning disability for the last eighteen years and contributes to the training of art psychotherapists. She is a British Association of Art Therapists' approved clinical supervisor and private practitioner. Sandra is currently Senior Art Psychotherapist with the Specialist Learning Disability Health Team in Harrogate (Tees, Esk and Wear Valleys NHS Foundation Trust) where she has worked since 1992.

Foreword

Valerie Sinason

It is part of the generosity of spirit of this book that a poet and verbal psychother-apist has been invited to write the foreword. Although not an artist, as a child and adult psychoanalytical psychotherapist in the field of trauma and disability I have profoundly benefited from the multiple contribution of artists and art therapists to this field as co-therapists, supervisors, supervisees, illustrators, exhibitors and sharers and enrichers of cultural and clinical space.

Stephanie Bull and Kevin O'Farrell have provided us with an important and much-needed book. It is a significant addition to the small but growing library of books about therapeutic approaches to people with intellectual disabilities. Together with their contributors they have succeeded in reviewing the key areas of vulnerability, loss, dependency, shame, hope, fear, violence, stigmatising and creativity. They have examined these processes intrapsychically, environmentally and politically from a range of clearly described theoretical perspectives, always making sure that the subject's voice is heard and respected and that theory is an aid to understanding rather than a dissociative defence.

The very apt subtitle, 'Don't guess my happiness!' which comes from Adam's heartfelt narrative (movingly deconstructed by Kevin O'Farrell), informs the whole emotional atmosphere of the book. This is a union between person-centred and psychoanalytically informed truth-telling. It offers powerful support for a true self freed from the mask of secondary handicapping processes inflicted by society and internalised.

Within a carefully drawn inner and outer landscape the authors also delineate the significance and contribution of art therapy. The artwork within the book highlights the specific historic importance of this book as well as its generosity. Whilst the number of key therapeutic books in the field of intellectual disability is small enough on its own (and I feel most honoured by the use made of my own work), the number of books in this field from an art therapy perspective is even smaller (Rees 1998). This makes the book doubly important and welcome.

As Kevin O'Farrell and Stephanie Bull, the co-editors, have hoped, the book fulfils its aim of making the topics accessible to a large lay audience as well as to clinicians. It is helpful to any member of a multiprofessional team who would like to understand more about intellectual disability, as well as to anyone who would like to understand the use of art therapy as a medium of processing feelings and development.

Stephanie Bull educates the reader about the government acts and interventions in order to illustrate the political environment and its impact, a review given extra power by her interview with a service user, Matthew. Jane Caven clinically and theoretically looks at the meaning of the Phantom of the Opera's scar and mask in her respectful clinical work whilst Kim Dee examines the central issues of loss and bereavement with sensitivity. There is also a report from a carer, Janet, a voice that Kevin O'Farrell is concerned is under-represented in our work.

Physical disability is explored honestly by Stephanie Bull and Emma Shallcross, with a focus on the meaning of a shunt, literally and symbolically, in one young woman's life and how it allowed a grief process to be worked through. Stephanie Bull also explores how making a 'beast' aids a man in dealing with the monstrous projections from society. Rather generously, this book also cares for the verbal as well as the pictorial. Indeed, Sandra Storey uses a Gillian Clarke poem and traces verbal improvements too. Sandra Goody tackles the emotional minefield of infantalisation and dependency from a range of clinical and theoretical perspectives. Jo writes about fear and anger whilst Elizabeth Ashby provides clinical and theoretical understanding about fear and violence in the counter-transference. Quentin Bruckland writes about powerlessness and shame together with epilepsy.

As well as the leitmotif of art, we can also see here the way in which themes become stronger through being echoed in different ways by the different contributors, thanks to the careful selection made by the co-editors.

Why is this book so useful and important for professionals who are not art trained? Perhaps we are all growing more enculterated into ideas of choice, multiplicity and the need, especially with vulnerable populations, for providing a richness of multiple interventions to make up for deprivation. One of the advantages of working in the field of intellectual/learning disability is that we all share an awareness that no one method is the only answer. No one can grow out of a disability. However, with attuned respectful bearing-witness, quality of life can improve immeasurably.

Although psychiatrists, social workers, nurses, psychologists and adult psychotherapists and counsellors working with the non-intellectually disabled adult population largely use words, those who work with vulnerable populations are also more aware now of the help art can provide. For example, extremely traumatised, disabled and tortured adults might find it easier to draw or make what has happened than to speak it. Neuroscience is also showing us the way creative activity can aid traumatic states in ways verbal interchanges do not.

Professionals working with children, of course, have always been aware of the crucial importance of art even where the art has been seen as a transitional space to aid other development rather than appreciated and understood in its own right. This book helps the non-artist appreciate the meaning of the actual making, doing, the issues of joining left and right brain, the harnessing of conscious and unconscious processes.

In my disability work at St George's Hospital with Professor Sheila Hollins we became deeply aware of the importance of art in providing access to emotions even though we were not art therapists. Indeed, at various times in the lives of the long-term psychotherapy groups for adults with an intellectual disability we invited art therapists to come in and be co-therapists for several sessions. I will never forget my surprise, not just at the visual depth of what was created or the impact of the actual physical, mental and creative task in making something, but at the way that one man, relentlessly troubled by flashbacks that drove him to psychosis, was able to be verbally clearer than we had ever heard him whilst his brain and soul were occupied with his painting.

My reading of the book also reminded me of the time a disability art therapist, Deborah Stickland Evans, helped the multiprofessional, highly verbal team make clay masks in our weekly staff supervision workshop so we could personally see and experience the pleasure in making. She later developed a charity, Outside In, to help people with intellectual disabilities go to museums and art galleries to internalise culture in a way they are all too often deprived of. As she told us, exposure to art and culture is important to *everyone's* sense of social identity and well-being. At St George's, we also saw the way psychotherapy work was made easier by the *Books Beyond Words* series which were indeed beyond words. They were pictures. However, they had been specially placed to form a narrative that could be understood. A whole range of important issues could suddenly be opened up using the transitional space of art contained within the shape of a book.

The way art can both provide space and enrich just by being art, as well as the use of art as a therapeutic medium, was also brought home to me in a combined way by a moving presentation by the artist Kim Noble and the art therapist Ami Woods at the BAAT annual conference in London, April 2011. As well as showing slides from Kim's recent exhibitions, Kim and Ami spoke about their group at Springfield Hospital for people with mental health problems and people with physical and intellectual disabilities.

Art in all its forms is part of a cultural history of intellectual disability. As a child, I would hear my father, the late Professor Stanley S. Segal, speak forcefully on the destruction to the spirit and corrosive shame caused by poorly illustrated books for children and adults with an intellectual disability. With his *Space Age Readers* he attached the social significance and excitement about Yuri Gagarin and the Sputnik to brightly coloured books so that his E-stream class would not be shamed. In his pioneering school and residential community work he became aware very early on that creativity was a precious human resource and that art and music could access feelings and communications in children and adults with intellectual disabilities in a very different way than words did, and sometimes in a more profound way (Segal 1967, 1991).

This book contains pictures and words together. It also holds cries, screams, shy smiles, a flutter of hope, the shame of a scar. In combining theory and practice, words and art, thinking and feeling, it provides the possibility of reaching for a true feeling whether of happiness or sadness.

References

Noble, K. (2011). *All Of Me. The Extraordinary Story of the 20 Personalities Who Share My Body*. London: Little Brown/Piatkus.

Rees, M. (ed.) (1998). *Drawing on Difference: Art Therapy and People with Learning Disabilities*. London: Routledge.

Segal, S. S. (1967). *No Child is Ineducable*. Oxford: Pergamon Press.

Segal, S. S. (ed.) (1991). *Creative Arts and Mental Disability*. London: A. B. Academic.

Acknowledgements

We would like to thank Adam, Matthew, Patrick, Paul, Sarah, Leila, Henry, Judy, Ruth, George, Catherine, Jo, Tony, Cheryl, Laura, Thomas, David B and William for letting us share their words and stories.

We would also like to thank the following people for their support and contribution to this book: Phil Province, Sharon O'Farrell, Zoë Cohen-Bull, Stan Roman, Dr Matt Symes, Cliff Free, Chris Peckham, Margaret Hill, Marian Liebmann, Valerie Sinason, Karen Fricker, Dave Fergusson, Dave Smallman, Richard Bateman, Neil Springham, Val Huet, Barrie Damarell, Frances, Maz and Marian at Hawthorn Lodge Library, Stella Scott at Rufus Lodge Library, Simon Hackett, Hannah Davison, Steve Cavill, Eileen Chapman, Matt Ring, Kathy Blair, Brian and Juliet Bull, Lorna Bryce, Mary Beavis, Julie Lunt, Phoebe Roman, Stella Joel, Bev Pearson, Terri Nolan, Laura Brummer, Carol Grey, Frankie Broadway, Suzanne Dominy, Hilary Linsen, Julia Brewin, Dominic White, Nicole White, Dr Cheryl Jones, Ari and Chris Szabo-Hemmings, Naomi Insley, Cate Holness, Pip Coker, Harriet Salzman, Joy Dee, Dora and Darko Mocilnikar, Terry Malloy, Suzanne Wilson, Asha Davis-Jama, Angela Charrington, Robin Tipple, and the numerous colleagues and managers within Southern Health NHS Foundation Trust who have supported and encouraged us.

The cover painting is 'Windows' by Jim Winteridge. With kind permission of Dr Micha and Jayne Jazz.

'Don't guess my happiness!'

Adam

'Well what I want to say is, when I was born I didn't breathe properly because I just didn't breathe and, now I'm older, because I couldn't breathe, I got a disability and I have people helping me but, when they help me or they think they're helping me or they say sorry or they help me do the house stuff or the shopping, it really doesn't help me at all because they say sorry or I'm doing well but I'm still aggressive and I'm still angry and it's not I'm being cruel, the fact is, what they're teaching me or think they're teaching me is a load of crap.

. . . My friends, my family, my relations, they always treat me their shit and I'm so fucking pissed off and upset with it. It doesn't matter what they do or how they say it, what they say to me, they either ignore me, they say sorry, or you've got to do it this way, or you're doing well. It is so full of fucking shit. I want to be an actor, I want to be a singer, I want to learn how to drive and I want to be able to read scripts. All I'm being taught is their fucking shit all the time . . .

. . . Why do people love me being aggressive? Why by saying sorry is that going to help me? Why do they think by learning their way that they're helping me? Why do they think they're going to think their way is going to make me do better, cos I can't see me ever being happy because their way is so full up their own arse? My head is so wound up with their shit that I can't learn anything because my head is so full of fucking shit that I don't even know what I'm doing or where I'm going, let alone what I'm going to learn.

. . . All I want to do is to learn how to read and write, learn to sing, learn to drive and learn scripts and stuff so I can get a PC for myself so I can play games and do photographs and do real photography and have the internet and famous and all that but they say, "oh no, sorry" and "how about this instead" and I say, if they're going to say that, I'll say fuck off why do you bother . . . It's sort of like the game Monopoly . . . As soon as you go onto Mayfair or Pall Mall – you pay and then you're okay but if you try and do something for yourself, it's "oh sorry – you don't need that, you'll be alright without that", but [my Carers] come to help you but, the fact is, they're helping you or it's just, it's their way.

They'll listen to you but when they've listened to you it goes back to what they think is more important than you because, because they're older than you they know more than you. Don't listen to yourself, always them; it's always them, fucking them . . . It's not about my disability; it's more about what's in my soul and what's in my spirit. And all people are giving me is their fucking shit and they expect me to be happy. Don't ever come and try and help me your way cos it's so full of fucking shit.

   . . . I've tried to tell people that I'm unhappy but people, they don't want to know about my unhappiness, all they want to know is do what they feel is better for themselves.'

Introduction

Learning disabilities, art therapy and the common themes

Kevin O'Farrell

'Don't guess my happiness!'

'Don't guess my happiness!' was a working title for this book from the beginning. It was the deep cry of a young, charismatic man in his twenties trying to find meaning and purpose in his life. This powerful, well crafted statement was aimed at all of Adam's caregivers, including me, his art therapist. His angry, frustrated and compelling plea for happiness pulled at the braces of my being but what exactly did *he* mean by this statement? Whilst I tried to understand this within the therapy context I was also grappling to find a simple way to explain art therapy to senior managers. The combination of the two set me on a course I was not expecting.

How this 'simple' book began

The conception began with the word 'simple'; a six-letter word that hardly looks intellectual at all. The big day had arrived and there was one hour to go. I was already quaking in my polished shoes and anxiously seeking out a second cup of coffee. Was what I'd prepared to say simple enough for the occasion? The danger would be to over-complicate the subject matter and bore everyone to death. Art therapy has a history of working with complex cases and in learning disabilities this is no different, though perhaps not so recognised. I needed to employ and trust in the qualities of this six-letter word more so than I had ever done before. 'Keep it simple and interesting' I kept repeating to myself. This presentation to senior NHS managers on 'What is art therapy?' in less than 20 minutes was like going on safari to meet the big game. It felt both exciting and deadly serious. However, having such an opportunity helped me outline a simple way of communicating what we did.

For a number of years I had been trying to capture the main themes that I'd come across working in learning disabilities and was slowly beginning to develop what is referred to as the 'spider' diagram (see Figure I.1). I began discussing these themes with my colleagues, Stephanie Bull and Dr Matt Symes, Clinical Psychologist. I then checked these out by attending some training facilitated by the Art Therapy Learning Disabilities Specialist Interest Group (ATLD SIG). All

Common themes

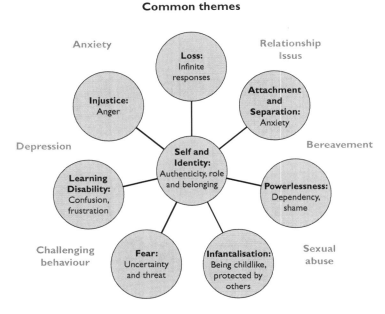

Figure 1.1 Common themes.

the themes were present but in no particular order. I simply found myself categorising them and, through discussions with Stephanie, the thought of writing a book was born. Almost immediately we knew we wanted to capture the voice of people with learning disabilities as much as we possibly could. In addition we realised that there had been no new art therapy publication addressing this landscape in the past twelve years. We tentatively put our feet into the publishing pool and waited to see what ripples would bounce back.

From Mair to here

Mair Rees (1998) concludes in *Drawing on Difference* that it would be beneficial within supervision to identify common or recurring themes for art therapists who work with people with learning disabilities. In part, this book is an attempt to map out common themes implicit in the world of learning disabilities. Through case studies, a variety of art therapists from newly qualified to very experienced, share their observations, thoughts and experiences about these common themes. While the case studies will be beneficial to clinical supervision, this book is written with caregivers, managers, trainees and the interested reader in mind. This book, like a baby, was an unplanned pregnancy. Similar to Rees, Stephanie and I were expecting somebody more academic than us to have taken up the pen, and a new book seemed mysteriously overdue.

So what has changed since 1998?

As well as electronic technology there have been some big changes since *Drawing on Difference*. For art therapists, there has been the shoring up of professional boundaries with state registration and the making of supervision obligatory. Art therapy is now part of the Health Professions Council (HPC) which regulates, protects and audits the profession.

In terms of the learning disability landscape, many significant changes have been instigated by the litany of new policies and legislation passed under the Labour Government (1997–2010). In Chapter 1, Stephanie Bull discusses this in more detail, charting the prolific increase in policy making since the Human Rights Act of 1998. With new legislation has come new language, and in political circles there has been a shift from 'learning difficulties' to 'learning disabilities'. The latter is the term that will be used exclusively here. Much of this new language is embedded with a person centred focus and approach.

Postmodernism distrusts the voice of the author, as much as it questions the lone authority of a doctor. The case of Dr Harold Shipman, jailed for 15 murders in 2003, underlined this all too well. The domain of the professional has slowly been experiencing a redress of power towards the person centred philosophy. If 'service users' are now included in developing services, should it not also be the way forward for writing a book? Collaboration in many contexts is on the increase and is legitimised by a growing understanding and awareness of social inclusion. From the start, Stephanie and I wanted the voice of people with learning disabilities to be integral to the narrative of the book. For this reason the book is peppered with snapshots of real dialogue (including the title of this book) which are provided by people with learning disabilities.

'Don't guess my happiness!'

While this statement had meaning within therapy I found it also had a voice and significance outside of the art room. I shall attempt to unpack this in a systematic and philosophical way, beginning with 'happiness'.

It would appear that happiness has increasingly become a focus and goal of Western, contemporary society evidenced through politics, consumerism, literature and media. On 15 November 2010, the BBC website reported that the Office for National Statistics is to devise questions in the new government's plans 'to measure people's happiness'. On my desk sits the 2011 catalogue from home furnishings giant Ikea who suggest that happiness can be created by living 'a happier life at home'. The flat-pack acquisition of it is equalled by the plethora of television programmes, resources and books produced over the past decade. Gilbert (2007), Haidt (2006), Layard (2005), McMahon (2007) and Schoch (2007) to name just a few, have boldly published books with the word 'happiness' in the title. As adviser to the Labour Government Richard Layard was even crowned the 'Happiness Tsar' calling for a need to focus on general well-being (GWB) and not just on gross domestic product (GDP). In 2006, the film, *The Pursuit of Happiness*, was released lifting Thomas Jefferson's words from the American Declaration of Independence. Despite recent economic fragilities and uncertainties the quest and complexity of this search goes on. Indeed the leading character in this 2006 film comments on Jefferson's choice of the word 'pursuit', placing the emphasis on the opportunity, accessibility and the *right of everyone* to pursue it.

Arguably, 'Don't guess my happiness!' is Adam's message to service providers to do better. Over the last 100 years the philosophy of learning disability has been the domain of professionals, encompassing medical, behavioural, social and educational models (Kay 2003). Emerging now is the person centred, *rights* based philosophy and approach reflected in collaborative partnership boards, service user evaluation groups, person centred planning and social action participant researchers. In short, there has been a political shift in power where people with learning disabilities are being invited into the driving seat, to the extent that many now live as tenants and some have bought their own homes. This *right* extends to individuals getting married and having children together, formerly taboo subjects within learning disability (Sheppard 2003). Such choices and goals as these are sought because arguably they will bring a degree of happiness. The former 'duty of care' model now perches on a see-saw with the Mental Capacity Act (2007) which determines capacity and thereby legitimises the *right* to make even unwise choices. 'Unwise choices in whose eyes?' is the question that subsequently follows, challenging carers and professionals alike. It is a new and developing landscape.

Given the vast amount of diverse literature on how to achieve happiness and well-being we may conclude that there is no consensus on exactly what it is or how to achieve this state of being. Potentially this becomes even more difficult for people with learning disabilities when communication can be problematic and there are differences in exposure to life experience. As Kay reflects: 'Of course, the biggest challenge of all is actually identifying exactly what the aspirations, wants and needs are of those people who invite the professionals to participate in their support' (Kay 2003: 183). Having attended many person centred plans (PCPs) there are always suggestions made to the person, or in Adam's words, 'guesses'.

Rights, capacity to make unwise decisions, person centred planning, self-directed support and equality of access to services are all heralds of empowerment, but are they simply the best efforts and 'guess' of 'professionals' to appropriate happiness for people with learning disabilities? Is this empowerment, through policy making, the ultimate goal in the pursuit of happiness or is there something more we can and need to explore?

Mind the gap

If we listen more carefully, 'Don't guess my happiness!' could imply that Adam doesn't know what his happiness is or is not able to convey what it is. If he knew and could communicate effectively what it was, there would be no *gap* for care-givers to fill with their guesses. Alternately, it might mean that he knows exactly what his 'happiness' is and has been able to articulate this but nobody has been able to secure it for him. In both scenarios a gap exists and therefore invites guesses, in terms of what it is or how to pursue it. Caregivers, of course, will offer sensible guesses (i.e. choices or suggestions) about how to pursue the happiness goal. 'Unwise' choices are rarely experienced because they are highly unlikely to be presented to the person with a learning disability. The reason for this is that the predominant relationships for people with learning disabilities are of a professional, duty of care, nature where they are supported and therefore insulated by caregivers. The government's White Paper, Valuing People (Department of Health 2001) recognised that people are often socially isolated and more recent studies have continued to highlight low levels of 'friendship activity' (Emerson and McVilly 2004; Robertson *et al.* 2001; Stancliffe 2007). Thus, a top-heavy experience of carer relationships can potentially rob someone of making unwise choices and subsequently the ability to learn from mistakes. So even when wise choices or suggestions made by caregivers yield positive outcomes they are not necessarily experienced by the person as belonging to them. As Adam would tell me: 'I do what they think is best, I never learn for myself.'

The gap is filled with a smile

Consequently, this *gap* and the readiness to fill it can be a real source of pain and frustration particularly accentuated when it is not consciously recognised by either the person or their caregiver. In such contexts pretence and acquiescence can be employed because the frustration is all too often exhausting. For both therapist and person in therapy, I have noticed that smiling and joking will often follow a more serious discussion. Indeed, Sinason (1992) explained a phenomenon which she referred to as the 'handicap smile', which was related to loss and trauma. She describes this 'secondary handicap' as the response to the 'primary handicap' (i.e. the learning disability) and 'how it is not dealt with' (ibid.: 21). She provides a number of examples where the response to an unfavourable difference results in the collusion of both parties to smile. This implies that beneath the learning disability, for those with even a subconscious awareness, is the pain of difference; first experienced, perhaps, as a parent lovingly gazes into the child's eyes and nervously smiles. Within other health contexts, such as mental health, people are treated to recover but within learning disabilities, when the brain has stopped developing at the onset of adulthood, there is no recovery from the learning disability itself.

'Smile or Die' concludes Barbara Ehrenreich (2009) in her subtitled book: *How Positive Thinking Fooled America and the World*. In her treatment for cancer she was told she could simply defeat the disease with a positive mental attitude. When we avoid or deny pain we split off parts of our self and those we care for. It becomes even easier not to see the pain when those who struggle internally also find it easier to avoid because it is difficult to cognitively articulate. You smile, I'll smile. It hurts. I can't tell you exactly how. I find words difficult. If we both smile, things seem happy in the moment but when you're gone nothing has changed. I need you to return, so I don't want you to be unhappy. I don't want to upset you but I feel alone inside and still hurting. People may emphasise my rights and offer me choices but is there anyone who will hear my cry?

Of course, no one with a learning disability has, to my knowledge, been able to articulate such a definitive cry. Indeed there is research that concludes that people with learning disabilities have little awareness of the label but a literature review by Beart *et al.* (2005) concludes that many people do experience the stigma and emotional pain of their social identity 'through their interactions with others' (ibid.: 54).

In terms of 'interactions' with those who are responsible for defining this social identity, Sinason (1992: 43–46) observes and charts history's struggle to find a helpful label. She does this partly by presenting a 'brief linguistic history' of common words used to describe 'learning disability', listing some 40-plus words over the last 400 or so years. This means there has been a change on average every ten or so years. Currently, the term 'intellectual disability' is used in research contexts, mostly it seems on the other side of the pond, whereas here in the UK the term 'learning disability' is politically used although the term 'learning difficulty' is also in use. The term 'intellectual disability' might be considered a more accurate and evolutionary description because it implies the brain has the capacity for learning. Sinason, however, warns us of the historic pitfall that is hidden in the changing of terms. The consistent societal and behavioural need to find new words simply underlines the pain of something that, despite biological and neurological advances, cannot be cured. In the unapologetic and now, perhaps, uncomfortably entitled *Mental Handicap and the Human Condition*, Sinason reminds us (because generationally we've forgotten) that the first historical meaning of the word 'stupid' is to be 'numbed with grief' (ibid.: 43). 'Stupid' and other descriptions become contaminated, abused or associated with discrimination. In fact Sinason illustrates how the word 'discrimination', in earlier dictionary editions, implied both positive and negative meaning, but in later editions it is associated more specifically in the latter context and with prejudice against someone. It would appear that even words that have, or are elevated to, neutral status eventually and mysteriously become infected when they are associated with something painful or uncomfortable. This is, it seems, part of the 'human condition'. Somehow a distancing and hence a splitting-off occurs with the language, which if unloved turns into a stagnant pond. Words slowly drift and collect at the edges and die. We might reasonably conclude that 'learning disability' and 'intellectual disability' are the latest descriptions to parade popularity and subsequently ask the question: how long will they live?

Learning disability: what and who are we talking about?

What is learning disability? For me, it is a potentially complex question. All of us, if we can, will be tempted to reduce the answer to a simple description or image.

Our instinct to pigeon-hole and stereotype in order to help us make sense of a complex world is an economic tool we all use. However, let us suspend all assumptions. Instead, imagine a large, blank, white canvas in front of us waiting for some lines to be drawn. Very quickly I want to sketch an image for you of learning disability but, in creative fashion, I'm going to start by using a different perspective and style.

I often chuckle inside and take delight in the unique challenges and varied surprises that working as an art therapist regularly unveils. There have been several occasions, in the modest reception area where I am based, on which I have greeted the person with a learning disability and their 'carer' only to discover that my assumptions of who was who were greatly misplaced! Reeling with embarrassment that was only known to me, I was reminded again that you really cannot judge a book by its cover. One man epitomised this world of misconceptions one day when he turned to me and said: 'I'm telling you Kevin, it's not me who needs therapy, it's my Dad!'

I once worked with a man, of few words, who was reported missing to the police. So serious was the situation, with concerns for his vulnerability running high, that an appeal was made on the local six o'clock television news. Shortly after this a receptionist from the city's most prestigious hotel called to say he'd been staying there! It is surprising how persuasive owning a credit card can be for someone who'd ordinarily need to use Makaton (a form of sign language) to help him communicate. I also worked with a lady who flew to Australia on her own for a holiday, returning via LA.

While such individual stories are not so common I hope they challenge any quick and slick images that we may be tempted to employ in our thinking of what learning disability looks like or means. Indeed, I can be sure that you will have walked past someone with a learning disability in your local High Street and will never have known. Taken from their website, the British Institute for Learning Disabilities (BILD) informs us that a learning disability can be a useful label but *'people are always people first'*. It is the right of everyone to be treated as an individual. With this thought in mind, let us consider what is meant by this label.

A learning disability is caused by the way in which the brain develops and is generally categorised by a score of less than 70 on the IQ scale and/or by significant difficulties functioning with day-to-day activities prior to the age of eighteen. There are many forms but most develop before birth, during delivery or because of a serious illness in a child's early years. In researching this I was surprised to discover that, in terms of genetic causes alone, there are approximately 750 identified to date (Harris 2006: 103); the most recognisable likely being Down's syndrome. However, others are inexplicable and may be explained by problems at birth such as oxygen starvation to the brain or, as Sinason (1992) suggests, the result of child abuse and/or trauma. These causes all carry lifelong ramifications in terms of learning, understanding and communicating. Mencap estimates that there are 1.5 million people with a learning disability in the UK.

Mental health

Significantly, this group of people are very susceptible to mental health disorders. A review of the research estimates a prevalence rate of 27 to 40 per cent (Raghaven and Patel 2005: 38). Is this something particular to a learning disability population or, as Emerson and Hatton (2007) at the Institute for Health Research (Lancaster University, UK) conclude, something further to do with socio-economic disadvantages? Their extensive research of British children and adolescents with learning disabilities warrants our attention and highlights the need to address both the mental health needs of this group of people and their socio-economic environment.

The art therapy

The frustrated plea 'Don't guess my happiness!' could only mean putting aside one's preconceptions and working *with* someone. It's the kind of referral that forms the basis of going on a journey together within therapy as 'fellow travellers' (Yalom 2002: 8). Within art therapy this principally involves: providing and holding a safe therapeutic space and environment; learning someone's language through images, mannerisms, words, transference and counter-transference; facilitating someone's use and exploration of materials; offering new perspectives and ways for them to express and understand themselves; and, lastly, developing and equipping someone to engage with life outside the therapeutic relationship.

Unhappiness

Of course, working with someone in therapy generally means that they are experiencing a lack of well-being. 'Don't guess my happiness!' subtly implies that we may be focusing on the wrong thing. As it happened, Adam also wanted us to see his unhappiness and to take this seriously. The fact that caregivers were guessing his happiness caused him further frustration and led him to believe that nobody wanted to see his unhappiness. In turn, he felt he would never be understood. In this scenario one begins to realise that there are underlying issues which may never get addressed or attended to. It is a little known fact that underground peat bog fires can last for several months and even years without detection. To think exclusively about the surface landscape and guess anyone's happiness can be to miss something more poignant altogether. 'Happiness is always a delusion' concludes Stuart Jeffries in his interview with psychoanalyst Adam Philips who believes society's preoccupation with happiness is more of the 'problem rather than the solution' (in the *Guardian*, 19 July 2006). He tells Jeffries, 'The cultural demand now is to be happy, or enjoy yourself, or succeed. You have to sacrifice your unhappiness . . .'. It is forced underground. Adam would tell me that he would often pretend to be happy just to feel happy and to keep the people he relied on engaged in his life. Again we hear the echo of the 'handicap smile' (Sinason 1992).

If Philips' analysis of our cultural demand and obsession is even partly true, it does have some implications for people with learning disabilities who are largely dependent on the caregivers who provide such an influential circle of support. Therapy allows someone to express their unhappiness, work with it, share it, resulting in feelings of being heard and understood. However, the journey of therapy within the learning disability landscape has to navigate through a valley of powerful voices that, while nobly pursuing happiness for the 'client', may fail to recognise other internal narratives. The therapy journey with Adam took us underground, beneath the peat bogs, where fires hide and burn away. It was in following this deep vein that I began to understand and hear some of the common causes for unhappiness. However, the journey of therapy does not begin with these common themes but with the referral.

The peat surface: where referrals lie

Referrals come in all shapes and sizes and typically include: sexual and physical abuse, challenging behaviour(s), bereavement, relationship issues, anger management, eating disorders and self-harm. The list is not exhaustive. Such referrals are represented around the edges of Figure I.1 and they illustrate the surface layer. Whilst important, we argue that the resolution to such ailments must take into account the possibility that there may be fires burning under the surface. To light a fire on a peat bog is prohibited in some countries because it can burn underground, resurfacing metres away, long after the initial fire has visibly been treated and extinguished. It is very common for referrals that are associated with mental health and well-being to have a history. Very often one can trace similar referrals through current or archive files which strongly suggest that a fire is still burning. In some ways this veiled layer should come as no surprise because the majority of referrals are never made by the person but by professionals and their caregivers. In short it is a 'guess' and someone else's vision of the landscape. In an effort to broaden out this vision of the landscape, this book aims to map out the peat bog fires underneath the surface which we have called the 'common themes' and these are explored in Chapters 2 to 10 through case study examples.

The common themes beneath the peat

As art therapists who have worked with people for short and comparatively long periods, we have noticed some common themes that are ever present and burning under the surface. Kuczaq (1998) makes mention of two themes that he observed within art therapy. Both of these he relates to loss and one of these specifically to learning disability in terms of difference (ibid.: 156–161). Among the common themes that we have categorised, both loss and learning disability are included. By highlighting these themes we hope that all professionals, therapists, caregivers and providers will be more aware of what can lay burning below the surface and thereby able to engage people with better 'guesses'. For art therapists and students new to the landscape we hope that it will make for more effective and efficient therapy.

Each theme in this book relates and interconnects with each other and can be experienced at different levels of awareness. For example, fear may be a more subconscious theme that is acted out through behaviour, whereas injustice when given the opportunity can be a more conscious and well-articulated grievance. This also, perhaps, reflects the vastly different levels of ability and development that are categorised as ranging from 'severe' to 'mild' learning disability.

Lastly, we have tried to order each chapter chronologically, in terms of what might be experienced by someone with a learning disability. Despite being very rudimentary and certainly subjective we hope, nevertheless, that this creates some relationship and flow between the chapters.

Chapter 2: having a learning disability

We start with a person's awareness of their learning disability. No doubt this will begin in early childhood and will be punctuated by a number of subtleties, such as the attendance of a special school. This is particularly the case for those who remember being taken out of mainstream school one fateful day. Naturally, these subtleties become more apparent during late teenage years when peers or siblings begin to spread their wings, drive, attend university or find employment as observed by Davies and Jenkins (1997) in their research of transition to adulthood. At this point the difference can be brought into sharp relief. Some people of course may be able to accept and manage this, while for others it can be a real source of unhappiness and pain.

In this chapter Jane Caven writes about Patrick who used images from the *Phantom of the Opera* and *King Kong* to express the pain of feeling different. She explores whether and when it is important to address the learning disability and how to do this. Because difference can also be experienced as the loss of a 'normal' life, as inferred by Kuczaq (1998: 154), loss is the theme covered in the next two chapters.

Chapters 3 and 4: loss

When I think of loss, I'm instantly reminded of Helen (pseudonym) whom I saw in therapy for a very short time but whose first image remains engraved in my memory. On a large A2 sheet of paper she'd drawn 14 separate 'family' groups, recording each household she'd been a part of. Included in these losses and separations were birth parents, adopted parents, foster parents, other siblings, residential tutors and key workers.

Because of the breadth of this theme we decided to use two chapters to illustrate it. To introduce this Kim Dee gives an overview of the theory and existing literature on loss. This is followed by Kim's case study of Paul and the sensitive journey he undertakes in grieving for his father and making sense of death. Kim also demonstrates innovative practice by stepping outside of the classical art therapy role to enable the work to progress.

In Chapter 4, Stephanie Bull and Emma Shallcross consider the case of Leila who, having been physically abused by members of her family, was living at a 'safe house'. The discussion of one single image is presented as a transcript and gives the reader a flavour of the process within supervision.

Chapter 5: attachment and separation

One of the key features about loss, as the example of Helen illustrates, is the multiple separations that someone with a learning disability can experience. This is echoed in the exploration by Kuczaq (1998: 165) of 'learning to say "goodbye"', where 'trusting others proves so difficult' for the person in therapy. Often these separations have happened with very little notice or preparation. Emergency beds for crisis and placement breakdowns are part of the landscape. With such poor experiences of separation it is inevitable that this will significantly affect the process of forming new relationships. Helen attended all her sessions wearing a thick padded Michelin-Man-like jacket. It seemed to me that she so wanted a hug but at the same time was creating a protective layer against further loss and separation. All of Helen's losses began with the initial separation from her birth parents. The context here was unknown but insightful research has been done in terms of the effect and difficulties that a 'disabled' diagnosis of the child has upon the parents (Marvin and Pianta 1996, Oppenheim *et al.* 2007). In Chapter 5, Sandra Storey explores the dynamics between mothers and daughters where the quality of attachment and the experience of separation are so significant. She further explores the impact on George and the separations he experienced in a major change to his environment and home.

Chapter 6: infantalisation

Stack (1998: 102) drawing on the work of Bicknell (1983) encountered infantalisation with a 44-year-old man, who she struggled to remind herself was not a 4-year-old boy. It can be a very powerful phenomenon for the therapist. Bicknell infers that, for the parents, this process begins early on with the acceptance of the 'handicapped child' but the resistance to the 'handicapped adult' that is to come later (ibid.: 171). Respectively, we might also conclude that it is preferable for the child to remain a child, at some level, throughout their adult life in an attempt to remain accepted. This may also account for Stack's experience.

Sinason (1992) has also argued that a child may be 'stupefied' as a result of abuse and trauma. In my experience this phenomenon of becoming stupid can also be seen as a way of protecting oneself from further abuses and difficulties as well as blocking out painful memories.

In Chapter 6, Sandra Goody illustrates the theme of infantilisation in her case study of Catherine. The chapter shows that Catherine's mother thought that life outside the family was unsafe and unprotected. Of course, there is a reality of this for everyone but within learning disabilities there are good reasons to believe that protection is more warranted.

Injustice

Unfortunately, when Stephanie and I originally invited people to contribute to this book there was no one available to write on this theme. Those who expressed an interest were engaged in other studies and unable to commit the time. Therefore this theme does not appear as a chapter and so I give a brief overview here in the Introduction.

Adult safeguarding is now a significant focus of social services with many local authorities reporting an increase in referrals. Protection from abuse and bullying are high priorities within care and educational settings while a number of brutal murders within local communities have led to the codification of 'hate crime', section 146 of the Criminal Justice Act (2003).

No Secrets (Department of Health 2000), guidelines, protocols and training of care staff to spot and raise awareness are likely reasons for these increases but the statistics and developing legislation do illustrate the risk of abuse within the learning disability landscape. Research on the prevalence of the abuse of people with learning disabilities has become a growing concern (Beail and Warden 1995) but there are no clear figures. Williams (1995: 101–102) gives some reasons for this in the chapter and title of the book, *Invisible Victims*, considering the barriers to recognising and reporting crimes, including the invisibility of people with learning disabilities within care environments. Allegations and disclosures do not match the conviction rate. Many people that I have worked with are angry at the injustices they have suffered and are fearful of further abuses.

Incidences of institutional abuse were perhaps considered to be a part of a dark and forgotten past but the Cornwall (Department of Health 2006) and the Sutton and Merton (Department of Health 2007) reports serve as modern-day reminders of the acute need to combat this and to provide better strategies and guidelines.

In terms of bullying, there is reason to believe that children with learning disabilities are at higher risk of victimisation (Mishna 2003) and, for those adults with learning disabilities living in the community, charities such as Mencap continue to raise the awareness of 'hate crime' through their campaign, Living in Fear (2007).

Further injustice can be experienced by perpetrators with learning disabilities in the judicial system, in that they are disadvantaged. They are more likely to 'waive their rights', make false confessions to appease authority figures, be unable to meet bail requirements and are more generally convicted (Griffiths and Fedoroff 2009: 355). The Bradley Report (Department of Health 2009), a governmental review of the criminal justice system, also recognised the vulnerability and prevalence of people with learning disabilities within police custody, which it acknowledged could be quite high, estimating a figure near to 9 per cent (ibid.: 48–49). This over-representation is also recognised in the research of people with learning disabilities who sexually offend but are, notably, convicted for less serious crimes such as masturbating in public spaces, inappropriate touching and public exposure (Griffiths and Fedoroff 2009: 355). Furthermore, in comparison, people with learning disabilities are much more likely to be the victims than the perpetrators of sexual crime (Griffiths 2003: 677–690). Because there are many within the criminal justice system with a learning disability, providers, including the NHS, have responded to this with the creation of Forensic Services. This is an area that a number of art therapists work in. The experience of people with learning disabilities, both victims and perpetrators, inside and outside the criminal justice system, is one in which the threat of injustice is a very real and ongoing issue.

Chapter 7: fear

Mencap's campaign 'Living in Fear' (2007) highlighted the risk of injustice and abuse that may be experienced. However, fear can also exist on other more hidden levels. In this chapter, Elizabeth Ashby explores this theme through three different case studies. She explores how intrusive, paralysing and pervasive fear can be for everyone, including the therapist.

Chapter 8: powerlessness

This chapter considers the theme of powerlessness, which is possibly experienced more by those who have both communication difficulties and physical conditions such as cerebral palsy and epilepsy. Quentin Bruckland explores how feelings of powerlessness and shame were experienced by Thomas who lived with refractory epilepsy, and what impact this had on his self-identity.

Chapter 9: self and identity

If previous chapters have been eclipsed by a glacier of sweat and tears then this last case study beats out a rich deposit of hope. Stephanie Bull concludes with the fascinating case study of David B who has significantly contributed to the chapter in his own words. Searching for an authentic sense of self and identity is often activated when other issues and themes are worked through and therapy progresses. Bicknell (1983) considers the 'dawning' of sexuality as one of five significant life events for someone with a learning disability but for whom restrictions are often experienced. This case study charts the development of David B's sexual awareness alongside his confrontation with Down's syndrome through therapy and how he also found a sense of role and belonging.

References

Beail, N. and Warden, S. (1995) 'Sexual Abuse of Adults with Learning Disabilities', *Journal of Intellectual Disability Research* 39, 5: 382–387.

Beart, S., Hardy, G. and Buchan, L. (2005) 'How People with Intellectual Disabilities View Their Social Identity', *Journal of Applied Research in Intellectual Disabilities* 18: 47–56.

Bicknell, J. (1983) 'The Psychopathology of Handicap', *British Journal of Medical Psychology* 56: 167–178.

Davies, C. and Jenkins, R. (1997) 'She Has Different Fits to Me: How People with Learning Difficulties See Themselves', *Disability and Society* 12: 95–109.

Department of Health (2000) No Secrets. London: HMSO.

Department of Health (2001) Valuing People. London: HMSO.

Department of Health (2006) The Cornwall Report. London: HMSO.

Department of Health (2007) The Sutton and Merton Report. London: HMSO.

Department of Health (2009) The Bradley Report. London: HMSO.

Ehrenreich, B. (2009) *Smile or Die: How Positive Thinking Fooled America and the World*, London: Granta Books.

Emerson, E. and Hatton, C. (2007) 'Contribution of Socioeconomic Position to Health Inequalities of British Children and Adolescents with Intellectual Disabilities', *American Journal on Mental Retardation* 112, 2: 140–150.

Emerson, E. and McVilly, K. (2004) 'Friendship Activities of Adults with Intellectual Disabilities in Supported Accommodation in Northern England', *Journal of Applied Research in Intellectual Disabilities* 17, 3: 191–197.

Gilbert, D. (2007) *Stumbling on Happiness*, New York: Vintage Books, a division of Random House, Inc.

Griffiths, D. (2003) 'Sexuality and People with Developmental Disabilities: From Myth to Emerging Practices', in I. Brown and M. Percy (eds) *Developmental Disabilities in Ontario*, 2nd edn, Toronto, ON: Ontario Association on Developmental Disabilities.

Griffiths, D. and Fedoroff, J. (2009) 'Persons with Intellectual Disabilities Who Sexually Offend', in S. M. Saleh, A. J. Grudzinskas, J. M. Bradford and D. J. Brodsky (eds) *Sex Offenders: Identification, Risk Assessment, Treatment, and Legal Issues*, New York: Oxford University Press.

Haidt, J. (2006) *The Happiness Hypothesis*, New York: Basic Books.

Harris, J. (2006) *Intellectual Disability: Understanding Its Causes, Clarification, Evaluation and Treatment*, Oxford: Oxford University Press.

Kay, B. (2003) 'Changing Philosophy in Learning Disability', in A. Markwick and A. Parish (eds) *Learning Disabilities: Themes and Perspectives*, Edinburgh: Butterworth Heinemann.

Kuczaq, E. (1998) 'Learning to Say "Goodbye"', in M. Rees (ed.) *Drawing on Difference*, London: Routledge.

Layard, R. (2005) *Happiness: Lessons from a New Science*, London: Penguin Books.

Marvin, R. and Pianta, R. (1996) 'Mothers' Reactions to their Child's Diagnosis: Relations With Security of Attachment', *Journal of Clinical Child Psychology* 25: 436–445.

McMahon, D. (2007) *The Pursuit of Happiness*, London: Penguin Books.

Mencap (2007) Living in Fear.

Ministry of Justice (2003) Criminal Justice Act: HMSO.

Mishna, F. (2003) 'Learning Disabilities and Bullying: Double Jeopardy', *Journal of Learning Disabilities* 36, 4: 336-347.

Oppenheim, D., Dolev, S., Koren-Karie, N., Sher-Censor, E., Yirmiya, N. and Salomon, S. (2007) 'Parental Resolution of the Child's Diagnosis and the Parent-Child Relationship', in D. Oppenheim and D. Goldsmith (eds) *Attachment Theory in Clinical Work with Children*, New York: Guilford Press.

Raghaven, R. and Patel, P. (2005) *Learning Disabilities and Mental Health*, Oxford: Blackwell Publishing.

Rees, M. (1998) *Drawing on Difference*, London: Routledge.

Robertson, J., Emerson, E., Gregory, N., Hatton, C., Kessissoglou, S., Hallam, A. and

Lineham, C. (2001) 'Social Networks of People with Mental Retardation in Residential Settings', *Mental Retardation* 39, 3: 201–214.

Schoch, R. (2007) *The Secrets of Happiness*, London: Profile Books.

Sheppard, N. (2003) 'Relationship Issues: People with Learning Disabilities as Parents', in S. Hodges (ed.) *Counselling Adults with Learning Disabilities*, Basingstoke: Palgrave Macmillan.

Sinason, V. (1992) *Mental Handicap and the Human Condition*, London: Free Association Books.

Stack, M. (1998) 'Humpty Dumpty's Shell', in M. Rees (ed.) *Drawing on Difference*, London: Routledge.

Stancliffe, R. (2007) 'Loneliness and Living Arrangements', *Intellectual and Developmental Disabilities* 45, 6: 380–390.

Williams, C. (1995) *Invisible Victims: Crime and Abuse Against People with Learning Disabilities*, London: Jessica Kingsley.

Yalom, I. (2002) *The Gift of Therapy*, London: Piatkus Books.

Chapter 1

Personalisation and a new landscape for learning disability services

Stephanie Bull

Introduction

My first experience of working with people with learning disabilities was in 1992, when I was on placement within a therapeutic unit while completing my art therapy training. I got to know the people there as individuals and this challenged some of my preconceptions about learning disabilities. I also became aware of government proposals for change which were then primarily focused on closing down long-stay institutions and, instead, caring for people within community settings (House of Commons 1990). Since then, there have been significant developments in the provision of services for people with learning disabilities in the UK. The move towards personalised care and away from a predominantly service led approach has had a significant impact on the lives of many people with learning disabilities, particularly in the areas of accommodation, employment and social opportunities. In this chapter, I look at the changing political and social climate which provides the context for the case examples in this book.

I begin by looking at the significance of the government's White Paper, Valuing People (Department of Health 2001) and go on to consider some of the many documents that followed this. In selecting these documents, I have focused on the following themes:

- Health and well-being
- Dignity and safety
- Choice and control
- Inclusion and contribution
- Quality of life.[1]

This was partly because I felt they covered the key areas but also because I found that the sheer volume of documents was overwhelming and this was one way of making them more manageable. At the end of each section I have included a list of the key documents mentioned which I hope will be of particular benefit to students.

Finally in this chapter, I look at what is meant by the term *personalisation* and how this approach is likely to shape the way that services are provided in the future.

Valuing people

Drawing on Difference was published in 1998 (Rees 1998), the same year that the Human Rights Act was passed. This Act set out 16 Articles aiming to protect the dignity, safety, equality and freedom of all citizens regardless of ethnicity, gender, sexual orientation or disability (Department of Health, 1998). This opened the door to arguably the most significant government paper for people with learning disabilities since Better Services for the Mentally Handicapped (Department of Health and Social Security 1971*),* namely, Valuing People (Department of Health, 2001)*.*

Valuing People was promoted as 'A New Strategy for Learning Disability for the 21st Century' and aimed to bring about significant change so that people with learning disabilities could live full lives, be respected by their fellow citizens and expect the same opportunities as anyone else living in their community.

To do this it identified four key principles:

- That people with learning disabilities should have their legal and civil rights recognised.
- That independent living be promoted and supported.
- That people with learning disabilities be supported to make real choices about all aspects of their lives.
- That people with learning disabilities be included in mainstream society.

The government pledged to listen to people with learning disabilities on an ongoing basis and, to achieve this, 'Service User Groups' such as the National Forum for People with Learning Disabilities and the National Learning Disability Task Force were established. As a person centred approach to planning care was key, it was essential that social services and health services work together better to enable this to happen. Learning Disability Partnership Boards were set up across England and Wales. These were led by local councils and brought together all main services as well as representative people with learning disabilities with the objective of facilitating a person centred approach. In this way, all agencies became responsible for the care of people with learning disabilities.

Seven years later, The Joint Committee on Human Rights published A Life Like Any Other (House of Commons 2008). This report was based on an inquiry they had carried out into the extent to which the human rights of adults with learning disabilities in England were being respected.

Key findings were that:

- While Valuing People had provided a useful policy framework, the reality was that the human rights of adults with learning disabilities were still *not* being upheld.
- Public authorities were not fully committed to the implementation of Valuing People and any attempts to do so were undermined by limited resources.

It stated:

> The Committee recommends the introduction of a positive duty on public authorities to promote respect for human rights. Taking a positive and pro-active approach to the creation of a culture of human rights will encourage a move away from negative attitudes and stereotypes which have 'dehumanised' adults with learning disabilities in the past.
>
> (Joint Commission on Human Rights 2008)

At the time, the government was in the process of reviewing Valuing People and in 2009 Valuing People Now was published to explain this and set out an updated three-year plan (Department of Health 2009b).

Key documents

Human Rights Act (1998)
Valuing People (2001)
A Life like Any Other (2008)
Valuing People Now (2009)

Health and well-being

The World Health Organisation (WHO) defines health as 'a state of complete physical, mental and social well-being and not merely the absence of disease or infirmity'. This definition was formulated in 1946 and the fact that it included mental and social well-being was, at that time, a big step forward in people's thinking. There have been suggestions that this definition should be revisited and that it should now include a spiritual dimension as well (Larson 1996).

It is important to emphasise that the concepts of health and healthcare are not static and they have varied considerably from one culture to another as well as at different points in history. For example, in the West, the Cartesian view of regard-ing the body mechanistically was long established. There followed a significant paradigm shift in the 1970s when more holistic ways of thinking about health and healthcare became prevalent, where mind, body and spirit were considered to be completely interrelated (Capra 1983).

Within Valuing People, the government acknowledged that people with learning disabilities often struggled to maintain good health for a variety of reasons includ-ing disadvantage and discrimination. To address this, targets were set whereby all people with learning disabilities should be registered with a GP by June 2004 and have an individual Health Action Plan by June 2005.

A Health Action Plan is an individual plan drawn up by the person with learning disabilities and a health practitioner/facilitator (Department of Health 2002). Its primary purpose is to set out the actions required to maintain and improve the health of the person concerned. It was also thought that Health Action Plans would provide the opportunity to educate and inform the person and their carers about how to achieve and maintain good health.

In its report, Treat Me Right, Mencap (2004) argued that people with learning disabilities had poorer health than other people and were more likely to die early. It stated that a key factor for this was that people with learning disabilities received poorer health services. Within this report, Mencap described some real examples of people's experience of health services and identified areas where it felt change was needed.

Significant recommendations were as follows:

- That healthcare staff should have learning disability training.
- That health services should provide people with learning disabilities with services they need.
- People with learning disabilities should have longer appointments.
- Health information should be accessible.
- People's records should show if they have learning disabilities.
- Doctors should do more to look out for health problems in people with learning disabilities.
- Annual health checks should be offered.
- Other standard health checks should be offered, e.g. cancer screening.
- An inquiry should take place into why people with learning disabilities die younger.

(Mencap 2004)

Mencap followed this with another report called Death by Indifference (Mencap, 2007) which told the story of six people with learning disabilities – Emma Kemp (26), Mark Cannon (30), Martin Ryan (43), Edward Hughes (61), Tom Wakefield (20) and Warren Cox (30) – who all died prematurely as an alleged consequence of poor healthcare provision from NHS services. Mencap argued that with appropriate medical and clinical care their deaths could have been avoided and that this raised 'serious concerns' about the way in which people with learning disabilities are treated within our healthcare system. It stated that 'while health inequalities have been widely documented and the solutions clearly identified . . . nothing has been done'.

This report was designed to act as a 'wake-up call' for the NHS and it was even suggested that the 'government could face legal challenges under the new disability equality laws'.

Key findings were that:

- People with learning disabilities were seen as a low priority.
- Many healthcare professionals did not understand much about learning disability.
- Many healthcare professionals did not involve the families and carers – those people who often knew the patient best.

- Many healthcare professionals did not understand the law on capacity and consent to treatment.
- Health professionals relied inappropriately on their own estimates of a person's quality of life to formulate treatment plans.
- The NHS complaints procedure was often ineffectual, time consuming and inaccessible.

Mencap demanded from government that an independent inquiry take place and that these six cases be investigated together rather than separately. Mencap also demanded that improvement be made in the process of investigating complaints against the healthcare system (ibid.).

In its response to Death by Indifference, a report written by the government ombudsman entitled Six Lives: The Provision of Services to People with Learning Disabilities was presented to Parliament in February 2009. It called for an urgent review of health and social care for people with learning disabilities. The report revealed that there were some significant failures. It confirmed that, in one case, the person had died as a direct consequence of public service failure and that another of the deaths could have been avoided had the standard of care been better. Additionally, it had found that these people had experienced prolonged suffering and it acknowledged that their dignity had been hugely compromised. The report also highlighted the inadequate response to complaints made by family members following the death of their loved one.

Mental health needs

In addition to meeting physical health needs, Valuing People also stressed the importance of meeting the mental health needs of people with learning disabilities. People with learning disabilities are at greater risk of developing mental health problems than the general population (Hardy and Bouras 2002). In 2004, Green Light for Mental Health was developed by the Valuing People Support Team and the National Institute for Mental Health in England (Department of Health 2004). It was designed to act as a service improvement toolkit providing a framework for evaluating how well services were meeting the mental health needs of people with learning disabilities. It aimed to give an overview of what services should aim to achieve which included setting out government's expectations of services as well as looking at quality outcomes from the perspective of people with learning disabilities and mental health problems and their carers.

Key documents

Treat me Right (2004)
Death by Indifference (2007)
Six Lives: The Provision of Services to People with Learning Disabilities (2009)
Green Light for Mental Health (2004)

Dignity and safety

Just before the publication of Valuing People, a guidance document from the Department of Health was issued in March 2000 called No Secrets: Guidance on Developing and Implementing Multi-agency Policies to Protect Vulnerable Adults from Abuse (Department of Health 2000). This was produced in response to several serious incidents that had occurred highlighting the distance between the ideals of the Human Rights Act and the reality of life for some adults with learning disabilities. The aim was to develop a workable policy and framework for all organisations (e.g. police, health providers, social services and voluntary organisations) involved with vulnerable adults so that an effective multiagency response could be made where there were issues of concern or potential evidence of abuse in any setting. Preventing abuse whenever possible was of utmost importance but where incidents did occur then these agencies would need to demonstrate that they had 'robust procedures' in place for responding to them.

The document uses the following definitions:

> Vulnerable adult – *a person who is or may be in need of community care services by reason of mental or other disability, age or illness; and who is or may be unable to take care of him or herself, or unable to protect him or herself against significant harm or exploitation.*

> Abuse – *a violation of an individual's human and civil rights by any other person or persons. Abuse may consist of a single act or repeated acts and may be physical, verbal or psychological. It may be an act of neglect or an omission to act. It may occur when a vulnerable person is persuaded to enter into a financial or sexual transaction to which he or she has not consented or cannot consent. Abuse can occur in any relationship and may result in significant harm to, or exploitation of, the person who is subjected to it.*

> (Department of Health, 2000, drawing on Consultation Paper 'Who Decides' 1997)

It goes on to set out some guidance about when and how to intervene in such cases and how to assess the seriousness of any incident of abuse. Any assessment would need to be focused upon:

- the vulnerability of the individual
- the nature and extent of the abuse
- the length of time it has been occurring
- the impact on the individual
- the risk of repeated or increasingly serious acts involving this or other vulnerable adults.

Following the murders of Jessica Chapman and Holly Wells and the subsequent conviction of Ian Huntley, several recommendations were made within the Bichard

Inquiry Report (Bichard 2004). In response to these recommendations, the Independent Safeguarding Authority (ISA) was put in place and the Safeguarding Vulnerable Groups Act 2006 was passed (Department of Health 2006b). This was the legislative framework for a new vetting procedure. Where previously there had been three lists for people who were believed to be unsuitable for employment or voluntary work with children and vulnerable adults (POCA, POVA and List 99), there would now be just two. One list would hold the details of those barred from working with children whilst the other would hold the details of those barred from working with vulnerable adults. People could be on one or both of the lists. The ISA would act as a central service and decide who should and shouldn't be barred. It would continue to check and review who was and wasn't on each list to ensure that the lists reflected an accurate picture on an ongoing basis. To enforce this new system, several new criminal offences were put in place.

At about the same time, the Healthcare Commission (HC) and the Commission for Social Care Inspection (CSCI) carried out a joint investigation into learning disability services in Cornwall. A report of their findings was published in 2006 (Commission for Healthcare Audit and Inspection, 2006). The report painted a damning picture of widespread institutional abuse, poor standards of care generally and a reliance on the use of medication to control people's behaviour. The principles set out in the Human Rights Act and in Valuing People were not being adhered to and people's dignity and safety had been neglected. The following year, in 2007, the HC reported on an investigation of services in the Sutton and Merton Primary Care Trust (PCT) which identified similar concerns (Commission for Healthcare Audit and Inspection 2007). These reports then prompted a national audit of 200 NHS and private sector services for people with learning disabilities in England.

Unfortunately, this did not prevent ongoing systematic abuse from continuing in some care settings and, in May 2011, the BBC broadcast a *Panorama* undercover investigation into the mistreatment of adults with learning disabilities at Winterbourne View Hospital in Bristol. Four of the staff there were subsequently arrested on suspicion of assault and 13 were suspended.

The Care Quality Commission (CQC) which, in 2009, replaced the three preexisting commissions (CSCI, HC and MHAC (Mental Health Act Commission)) and whose job it was to inspect and monitor all care settings, had clearly failed to detect what was happening at Winterbourne View Hospital. Within 24 hours of the programme being broadcast, Dame Jo Williams, the Chair of the CQC, issued an unreserved apology, describing the failure as 'unforgivable' (guardian.co.uk 7 June 2011).

In an article for the *Guardian* (guardian.co.uk 1 June 2011), Professor Jim Mansell wrote that 'it isn't just about wicked staff or weak management. It is about the wrong model of care – people with challenging behaviour being shunted off to these institutions because their local health and social services have not got their act together to provide the kind of support they need locally.' He went on to say that 'the real solution though, is to stop using these kinds of place altogether'.

Hate crime

It is important that people with learning disabilities are equal members of their local communities and at the same time feel safe and properly supported as and when they need to be. Some, who want to live as independently as possible do not fully engage with services and can become extremely vulnerable as a consequence. The cases of Steven Hoskin (39), Brent Martin (23), Laura Milne (19), Keith Philpott (36) and Raymond Atherton (40) were reported nationally and tragically demonstrate the existence of hate crime against people with learning disabilities. These were all people who lived on their own in their local community. Some had contact with statutory services while others did not. They were all befriended by local youngsters who went on to viciously bully and exploit them over a considerable period of time and they were all eventually brutally killed by their persecutors. The difficult questions arise of how and when services should be involved with vulnerable people who want to live independently and who don't engage with services.

Managing risk

In experiencing greater independence and choice in their lives, people with learning disabilities also increase their vulnerability through reduced supervision and through taking up new opportunities for making choices, some of which might subjectively be regarded as unwise. The question of whether protection should be the overriding principle at the expense of independence and self-determination is an important one to consider and it is acknowledged that keeping adults with learning disabilities safe at the same time as maintaining the principles of Valuing People is a real challenge for services.

Clearly, to do anything in life involves a degree of risk and we are all unconsciously assessing and managing risk as we make decisions throughout the day. Today, a risk aversion culture, driven in part by fear of litigation and media focus, means that the completion of formal risk assessments dominates the work of many professionals within statutory services. Neill *et al.* (2009) argue in favour of a person centred approach to assessing and managing risk, suggesting that the person and their relatives be involved in the whole process. For example:

- Gathering information
- Defining the risk more precisely
- Thinking creatively about solutions
- Evaluating solutions
- Implementing actions.

A key point they make is that the 'purpose of any risk assessment is as much about the happiness of the person, their family and the community as it is about their safety' (ibid.).

Key documents

No Secrets (2000)
The Safeguarding Vulnerable Groups Act (2006)
The Cornwall Report (2006)
The Sutton and Merton PCT Review (2007)

Choice and control

The choices people make can of course range from the relatively trivial, such as which brand of coffee to buy, to the bigger decisions that have a much greater impact, such as where to live and with whom. Some choices are easily reversed while others have permanent consequences.

Actively making a choice is now usually seen as a positive thing to do in Western culture. However, it can become frustrating when options are very limited or it can be confusing when there are too many options. Making a choice about any aspect of one's life can be determined by a complex range of personal, cultural and experiential constraints and conditions.

When a person reaches the age of 16, current law states that they are able to make their own decisions about many aspects of their lives. They are considered to be competent and responsible enough to do so. Decisions relating to personal life, care, welfare and finances should always be made by the person concerned unless it can be proven that they do not have the capacity to do so. A Mental Capacity Assessment is required to determine that this is the case.

The Mental Capacity Act (MCA) was passed in 2005 and came into force in 2007 (Department of Health 2005b). It replaced previous common law about the treatment of people without capacity and made the presumption of capacity, unless proven otherwise, of primary importance. The Independent Mental Capacity Advocate Service was set up to assist vulnerable adults who do not have family and friends to support them, to understand important decisions that need to be made about their lives.

The MCA covers decisions relating to care, treatment and finances. Decisions such as whether or not to get married or have a sexual relationship or which political party to vote for can *never* be made by another person on their behalf. It is unlawful to neglect or to ill treat anyone who does not have capacity to make their own decisions. It is also important to recognise that a person's capacity to make any decision can vary from one point in time to another and that having capacity can vary from one decision to another.

If a potential lack of capacity for a key decision covered by the Act is identified, an assessment of capacity is required. The 'decision maker' would consult with the person, their family and other involved agencies to make a determination.

If it is assessed that a person does not have capacity to make any decision for themselves, the Act provides guidelines for appropriate professionals and carers who will need to make decisions on their behalf. Any such decision must be made in the person's best interest and in line with the guidelines that are set out in the MCA. People's freedom and human rights must be maintained as much as is possible.

Where there are complex cases or disagreement about capacity, a referral can be made to the Court of Protection for a judgment. The Court can appoint deputies to make a 'best interest' decision covering a specific area (ibid.).

An amendment to the MCA entitled Deprivation of Liberty Safeguards (DOLS) was issued in 2008. This was designed to provide a code of practice for those caring for very vulnerable people in a residential setting and to clarify when a person is, or is at risk of being, deprived of their liberty. It explains how deprivation of liberty can be avoided (Ministry of Justice 2008).

That people with learning disabilities be supported to make real choices about all aspects of their lives was, as previously mentioned, a key principle of Valuing People. However, 'choosing' can actually be quite a difficult thing to do for many people with learning disabilities. 'When the person making the choice does not feel in control of either the available options or the process by which the choices are made, reduced motivation is likely to lead to poor choices' (Harris 2003: 4).

There are often social and environmental factors that can have an influence on the way people with learning disabilities make choices. These can include:

- The behaviour of support staff – being directive and influencing choice rather than supporting and enabling choice.
- Service structures and resource limitations can mean reduced options for making choices.
- Communication difficulties.
- Fear of consequences if an 'incorrect' or unpopular choice is made.
- Routines that are inflexible.

Key documents

The Mental Capacity Act (2005)
Deprivation of Liberty Safeguards (DOLS) (2008)

Inclusion and contribution

The concept of *inclusion* for people with disabilities was first formalised when the 1970 Education Act was passed. This Act aimed to put an end to the idea that some children could never be educated. From this point on, all children were entitled to receive an education regardless of intellectual ability (Department of Education 1970). By 1978, the issue of integrating children with disabilities into ordinary schools was being discussed and the Warnock Report, investigating 'special education' was published (Warnock 1978). Inclusion, in all aspects of the lives of people with disabilities, is now driving government policy and changes in society.

In the UK in recent years there has been an aspiration for a more equal society where all citizens can expect to have rights, justice and life opportunities regardless of age, ethnicity, gender, sexual orientation and disability. It is important to recognise that being *equal* is very different from being *identical*. Equality recognises difference while still acknowledging fundamental similarities and rights that are a part of our common humanity and this is essentially the outcome that legislation is trying to achieve.

In 2005, the Disability Discrimination Act (DDA) was updated and extended beyond access to health and social services, as had been set out in the original Act in 1995 (Department of Health 2005a). The new Act covered employment, education, buying/renting property, functions of public bodies and access to goods or services. From 2005 all public bodies needed to ensure that they provided disabled people with equal opportunities and services. It required that institutions change and adapt their services to include people with disabilities rather than individuals adapting to the institution. This was a major shift and has led to structural modifications to buildings, changes in service delivery, and utilising a variety of ways in which to present information to people.

At the time of writing, the Equality Act 2010 is the latest of the government's moves towards a more equal society. Its main purpose is to bring together the key points of all discrimination legislation and includes the following areas:

* Direct discrimination
* Indirect discrimination
* Discrimination directly relating to disability
* Harassment
* Equal pay.

Key documents

The Disability Discrimination Act (1995 and 2005)
The Equality Act (2010)

Quality of life

Quality of life can sometimes be confused with such things as 'standard of living' or even happiness. Research literature identifies a combination of eight aspects of a person's life that play a part in determining the quality of life they experience:

* Interpersonal relationships
* Emotional well-being
* Material well-being
* Personal development
* Physical well-being
* Self-determination

- Social inclusion
- Rights.

(Adapted from Schalock et al. 2002)

How we quantify and evaluate a person's quality of life has proven to be difficult. Researchers have tried looking at both individuals and societies using a combination of measures such as life expectancy, education and material standards of living (e.g. the Human Development Index or the Physical Quality of Life Index). It is the more subjective elements such as personal development and emotional well-being that are more difficult to measure and consequently less reported on. In addition to this, people's aspirations (and therefore their expectations) in terms of quality of life are constantly increasing. This is especially true now within the learning disabled population.

In 2003, a social enterprise called In Control was formed by a small group of people from various organisations. It has since become a limited company and a registered charity. Its mission has been to work in partnership with other organisations to help people with learning disabilities achieve authentic choice and control in their lives. In Control believe that making changes in the social care system was essential and that making the concept of self-directed support (people assessing their own needs and making decisions about their support) a reality would ultimately lead to improving people's quality of life. To achieve this they set out a seven-step model:

- An individual budget is set.
- The person develops their own support plan of services that they want to spend their budget on (this would need to meet the local authority eligibility criteria as well as show how the money would be spent).
- The plan is agreed by the local authority.
- Agreement is reached on how the budget is to be managed. This might be done by the person themselves or by their representative in the local authority.
- Support is organised by the person, their family or their representative.
- The person lives their life.
- A review takes place and appropriate changes are made if necessary.

The In Control model acknowledges that it is the combination of having a realistic budget with access to appropriate support and opportunities that will enable the person to make real choices and ultimately improve the quality of their life. Quality of life does, of course, overlap with all the themes covered so far in this chapter and leads me to the concept of *personalisation.*

Personalisation

> Personalisation is the process by which services are tailored to the needs and preferences of citizens. The overall vision is that the state should empower citizens to shape their own lives and the services they receive.
>
> (HM Government 2007: 33)

Essentially, *personalisation* says that rather than fitting people to existing services, services should fit the person. It means that we begin with the individual, we consider their strengths and preferences and we include any existing positive support network of friends and family members. Personalisation means that we recognise that the individual is the person best placed to know what it is they need and how best their needs should be met. It allows people to take responsibility for themselves and ensures that appropriate information and support is available to enable them to do so.

Many social workers and health practitioners would argue that personalisation has underpinned their approach for many years but because the policy framework was not in place, delivering personalised services was often an uphill struggle. It was argued that personalisation would never be fully achieved without fundamental changes to the model used for service provision.

For many years, the model of the 'Professional Gift' has guided service provision:

- Society is taxed by government.
- Government distributes a portion of the money raised to local authorities.
- The local authorities set their own priorities and then allocate funds to different departments.
- Social services (one of the departments) are allocated funds from local authorities.
- Social workers and care managers assess needs and allocate services to those they feel need them most.

An alternative model has been put forward as a fairer way of providing services. This is known as the 'Citizenship Model':

- People requiring support are regarded as important members of their community who can be supported by their community.
- People are supported to assess their own needs.
- When required, the person can negotiate with 'Purchasers' and 'Providers' to ensure appropriate resources and support are available to the person.

Duffy states that 'it is important that the system of service delivery does not deliver support in a way which limits, controls and weakens the individual or cuts them off from their community but, instead, enables the individual to be a full citizen of the community' (Duffy 1996: 14).

This view was reinforced when, in January 2006, the White Paper, Our Health, Our Care, Our Say: A New Direction for Community Services was published. It set out four 'big ideas':

- Individuals would take responsibility for maintaining their health and well-being and better information would be available to enable them to do this.

- Services would really listen to what people were asking for.
- Services would be easier to access with more venues and convenient appointment times.
- People requiring long-term care would be more able to make choices about the services they were receiving. Multi-agency working and planning support for people would improve.

This White Paper promoted the use of direct payments and individual budgets to enable more individually tailored services. Its key purpose was to shift services from secondary to primary care (Department of Health 2006a).

The following year, in 2007, a government programme called Putting People First began (HM Government 2007). It set out the direction for adult social services and the way care would be organised. The programme claimed to be co-produced, co-developed and co-evaluated, meaning that people with learning disabilities were involved at every stage in the process. It identified four key areas for development in order to enable services to become more personalised:

- Universal services (e.g. health, education, transport, leisure, housing).
- Early intervention and prevention (i.e. provide the support needed to enable people to live independently for as long as possible).
- Choice and control (i.e. 'needs led' not 'service led').
- Social capital (i.e. people to access support from friends, neighbours and community resources).

Personalisation has several different elements to it and this can become a little confusing at times. It can involve a combination of any of the following:

- Having a personal budget allocated by social services.
- Self-directed support.
- Direct payments – where a cash payment is made directly to the person so they can purchase their own support rather than having to go through the council.
- In Control – using the seven-step model.
- Person centred planning – the practical part of personalisation. The person concerned is always at the centre of any decision making and actively contributes to planning future support.
- Support planning – when person centred planning is combined with a person's personal budget.

Talking to my colleagues from both Health and Social Services, the principles of personalisation are, of course, welcomed. However, some important questions have been raised such as:

- Will there be enough resources available for everyone needing services to have a sufficient individual budget?

- Will support vary from one area to another, i.e. will there be a postcode lottery?
- What happens with vetting procedures such as Criminal Records Bureau (CRB) checks if people are purchasing their own support?
- What if care needs change?
- What if people are persuaded by family members to let them provide the support when it is not suitable or appropriate?
- Will personalisation work for everyone?

Conclusion

Since my placement in 1992, the landscape for learning disability services has changed a great deal and will no doubt carry on changing until I have retired and beyond that. At the time of writing, the new Coalition Government has been in office for a year and their White Paper, Equity and Excellence: Liberating the NHS was published in July 2010 (Department of Health 2010a). This paper sets out reforms which, perhaps most significantly, include the devolution of commissioning responsibilities to GPs and their practice teams working in consortia. The full impact of this paper for learning disability services is still to properly emerge although we all know that, once again, big changes in the way that services are structured and provided are inevitable.

Have things really changed that much for art therapists who work with people with learning disabilities? Like all art therapists working within statutory services, we have, on an ongoing basis, needed to be creative to find ways of managing change and uncertainty in order to survive. We have always worked with the person at the centre and so 'person centred' working is not new to us. The individual narrative that has been such a vital aspect of our work continues to be so and our ability to give people with learning disabilities a voice where it may have been almost impossible to find a positive means of expression has not changed.

Art therapists will need to continue to be flexible in the way in which they present art therapy to other professionals and to managers. We will need to evidence, measure and explain our practice in a language that they can understand. However, whatever may be happening around us, it is imperative that we never lose sight of our primary task and focus which is always the person in therapy and the narrative that they bring.

Note

1 These themes were first used within the Department of Health's Position Paper Making Policy Count (Department of Health 2009a).

References

Bichard, M. (2004) The Bichard Inquiry Report. Cambridge. HMSO.
Capra, F. (1983) *The Turning Point*. London. Flamingo.

Commission for Healthcare Audit and Inspection (2006) Joint Investigation into Services for People with Learning Disabilities at Cornwall Partnership NHS Trust. London.

Commission for Healthcare Audit and Inspection (2007) Investigation into the Service for People with Learning Disabilities Provided by Sutton and Merton PCT. London.

Department of Education (1970) Education Act. London. HMSO.

Department of Health (1998) The Human Rights Act. London. HMSO.

Department of Health (2000) No Secrets – Guidance on Developing Multi-agency Policies and Procedures to Protect Vulnerable Adults from Abuse. London. HMSO.

Department of Health (2001) Valuing People. London. HMSO.

Department of Health (2002) Good Practice Guidance on Implementation for Learning Disability Partnership Boards. Pp. 5–6. London. HMSO.

Department of Health (2004) Green Light for Mental Health. London. HMSO.

Department of Health (2005a) The Disability Discrimination Act. London. HMSO.

Department of Health (2005b) The Mental Capacity Act. London. HMSO.

Department of Health (2006a) Our Health, Our Care, Our Say. London. HMSO.

Department of Health (2006b) Safeguarding Vulnerable Groups Act. London. HMSO.

Department of Health (2009a) Making Policy Count. London. HMSO.

Department of Health (2009b) Valuing People Now. London. HMSO.

Department of Health (2010a) Equity and Excellence: Liberating the NHS. London. HMSO.

Department of Health (2010b) Personalisation Through Person Centred Planning. Pp. 3, 33–38. London. HMSO.

Department of Health and Social Security (1971) Better Services for the Mentally Handicapped. London. HMSO.

Duffy, S. (1996) *Unlocking the Imagination*. London. Choice Press.

Government Equalities Office (2010) The Equality Act. London. HMSO.

Hardy, S. and Bouras, N. (2002) 'The Presentation and Assessment of Mental Health Problems in People with Learning Disabilities'. *Learning Disability Practice* 5, 3: 33–38.

Harris, J. (2003) 'Time to Make Up your Mind: Why Choosing is Difficult'. *British Journal of Learning Disabilities* 31: 3–8.

HM Government (2007) Putting People First: A Shared Vision and Commitment to the Transformation of Adult Social Care. London. HMSO.

HM Government Policy Review (2007) Building on Progress: Public Services. P. 33. London. HMSO.

House of Commons (1990) The NHS and Community Care Act. London: HMSO.

House of Commons (2008). A life like any other. London: HMSO.

Larson, J. (1996) 'The World Health Organization's Definition of Health: Social Versus Spiritual Health'. *Social Indicators Research* 38, 2: 181–192.

Mencap (2004) Treat Me Right. London.

Mencap (2007) Death by Indifference. London.

Ministry of Justice (2008) Deprivation of Liberty Safeguards. London. HMSO.

Neill, M., Allen, J., Woodhead, N., Sanderson, H., Reid, S. and Irwin, L. (2009) 'A Positive Approach to Risk Requires Person Centred Thinking'. *Tizzard Learning Disability Review* 14, 4: 16–23.

Parliamentary and Health Service Ombudsman (2009) Six Lives: The Provision of Public Services to People with Learning Disablities. London. HMSO.

Rees, M. (ed.) (1998) *Drawing on Difference*. London. Routledge.

Schalock, R., Brown, I., Brown, R., Cummins, R., Felce, D., Mastikka, L., Keith, K. and Parmenter, T. (2002) 'Conceptualization, Measurement, and Application of Quality of

Life for Persons with Intellectual Disabilities: Report of an International Panel of Experts'. *Mental Retardation* 40, 6: 457–470.

Warnock, H. M. (1978) Committee of Inquiry into the Education of Handicapped Children and Young People. London. HMSO.

Talking about learning disability services

Matthew

What do you think you expect from your life now that you didn't 15 years ago?
That is a hard question; it depends on what is out there in life.

It is nice to have paid work.

It is nice to be in control of my own life and my destiny.

Do you think that Health and Social Services are different now? If so, why do you think that is?
They are more modern now.

Their approach is a lot different to 15 years ago. There are PCPs (Person Centred Plans) now, before it was just what you were capable of.

What does 'Valuing People' mean to you?
It means people being in control of their lives and more and more people are now able to decide what they want for their lives. And also, it helps people and public bodies and community groups to work together in getting the best for people.

What does 'Person Centred Planning' mean to you?
It means you are able to change things and do things you have maybe never done before.

People can change their lives so much, like going on holiday trip, getting their own place, getting a new or different job.

People working together to get the best for other people.

Do you think that healthcare for people with learning disabilities has improved in the last 15 years?
It's a difficult one, it depends on the situation. Overall, they have tried to improve it but it doesn't work for everybody. There is more opportunity to find better ways now and having the right guidance.

Do you think that people with learning disabilities are safer these days?
Depends where they are living and all sorts of situations, where they work or go to college.

I feel safer because there are more police on patrol, more community help. But it's not always good for everyone.

Hate crime has been going on for generations and probably will go on for generations.

Do you think that information about what people like nurses and care managers are trying to do is easier to understand these days?
No – I think it's still as difficult and needs a lot of improvement in that area.

Bodies need to work together and make it understandable to the individual and not stereotype.

Do you think life feels more equal now compared to 15 years ago?
It's a lot better but needs to be a lot more improvement. Long way to go to make it perfect and that is for everybody, like elderly people and people from other backgrounds.

Do you think you are happier now than you were 15 years ago?
Some things are better, some things aren't. Work/college wise it's better. There were no jobs 15 to 25 years ago, only sheltered workshops.

In 1995 things were starting to improve and by 2000 onwards it was better for my work situation. Some things you gain, some things you lose.

Any other thoughts?
People are able to get together and for example, chair groups and have a forum for discussing things, and make more improvements. Like a watchdog to make sure things are happening. In hospitals and colleges they are learning to treat people better.

Need watchful eyes to keep everything in order.

I think having your own budget will help as people will choose the support they need.

For a lot of people who would not get to meet people with learning disabilities and carers it is an eye-opener and they are able to try and make the right decisions, without that they don't really have a lot of knowledge.

I think it is important to keep these groups going to see what is going on monthly.

Part I

Having a learning disability

Chapter 2

Having a learning disability
The question of what to say and how to say it

Jane Caven

Introduction

In this chapter I look at what it might mean to have a learning disability. I consider this in the context of why people with learning disabilities are referred for art therapy within the large community team of the inner city borough where I work, and their presenting issues. I look at other art therapists and psychotherapists who have written on the subject. The theory found includes an exploration of counter-transference responses to working in therapy with people with learning disabilities and what can be learnt from this about them. I consider the issue of addressing the learning disability in therapy and how we do this. I will give an example of a case study where some painful issues about having a learning disability were explored through the medium of popular culture and particular characters, which were brought into the session by the client. In my experience, this has proved to be a very accessible and useful means by which many people with learning disabilities referred to art therapy have addressed their learning disability and gained insight into their feelings. I will be drawing on some of the psychoanalytic theory on popular culture.

What does it mean to the person with learning disabilities to have a learning disability? What is the experience of having a learning disability like? Of course this will be different for everyone. There is the obvious difficulty with thinking, more profound in some than others. There is also the emotional experience of having a learning disability; the grief of the loss of the 'normal' person that might have been and the difficulties with making secure attachments. There are also the ongoing challenges of living with the stigma attached to the condition. Understandably many people with learning disabilities have an indescribable amount of emotional pain to bear.

Reason for referral to art therapy

Thinking about O'Farrel's 'peat bog' analogy in the introduction to this book, there are many reasons for referrals to art therapy, but commonalities between referrals can be seen. In the art therapy service of the community team, people with learning disabilities are often referred for 'behavioural problems', with a suggestion that the underlying cause may be around a significant milestone/transition, e.g. from school to college, or family home to residential home, or the death of a parent. The referrer (who may be another professional in the team, a social worker or support worker, parent or friend of the person with learning disabilities, or the person themself) is unsure about the change in behaviour but realises there are some underlying emotional difficulties. Art therapy might be considered as a way for the person to express their feelings and try to be helped with understanding their emotional difficulties. What I often discover once the assessment/therapy process is under way is that a complex set of issues and difficulties is being expressed through the 'challenging behaviour'.

What is sometimes evident to me through what a person communicates either consciously or unconsciously in art therapy, is that they want their learning disability acknowledged and they want permission to explore their feelings about it. Valerie Sinason, who has written on the subject, states that if therapist and client continue to ignore the learning disability, then 'a handicapping process has begun' (Sinason 1992: 81). She describes psychotherapy sessions with people with learning disabilities in which she has been very direct and helped them to move forward in therapy. Personally I have often found that whilst the subject has been present in the room, it is sometimes difficult to know *how* to address it, without being starkly confrontational. As with the 'peat bog' analogy, if disability and pain are denied and split off they resurface elsewhere, and the underlying problem comes back at a later stage.

Some theoretical perspectives

Containment

The baby in the early relationship with the parent needs to feel contained for healthy development (Bion 1959, in Sinason 1992). This experience is likened to that of the person in therapy. The child's unbearable, painful feelings need to be tolerated, contained and made more manageable by the parent, so that they become bearable and anxiety does not develop in the child. As with the 'good enough' parenting (Winnicott 1971), 'containment is an essential prerequisite for any therapeutic change' (Sinason 1992: 81).

The loss of the perfect child

Commonly, parents of a child with learning disabilities will feel very disappointed and can experience grief for the loss of the 'perfect child' (particularly in infants where the learning disability can be seen at birth).

Marvin and Piñata (1996) develop Bowlby's (1980) ideas about the grief process, saying they can be applied when a child with learning disabilities is born.

The parents of a learning disabled child may not accept that their infant is learning disabled by continually searching for a reason, or may continue to hope that their child will 'recover', as part of the grieving process. They may feel guilt, imagining that they have caused the learning disability which can lead to over-protection and as the child grows this can have an inhibiting effect on development (Sinason 1992; Barnett *et al.* 2003).

'Having a learning disability': literature review

Szivos and Griffiths (1992) write about a group they ran for people who had mild learning disabilities and low self-esteem. The group looked at identity issues and loss associated with having a learning disability. They used Kubler-Ross's (1970) theory on the acceptance of loss, applying the different stages to the acceptance of learning disability, alongside the forging of a positive identity. The authors found that most members felt less rejected and more accepting of themselves by the end of the group.

Kuczaj (1998) discusses having a learning disability in relation to working with loss. He talks about 'similarity and difference' being a common theme in his work with people with learning disabilities. He says that this is associated with loss, and acknowledges how in therapy one can look at the differences between therapist and client, but that it is hard to address the aspect of disability. Kuczaj writes about a person with learning disabilities who compares himself with his therapist, wanting to be 'clever' like him. He says that for the person to accept that they have a learning disability, they have to let go of the hope they had of being like non-learning disabled people. Kuczaj cites Bicknell (1983) who considers what it means to have a learning disability: 'What does it mean, to this person, to have this handicap? At this time in his or her life? With these caretakers? In this environment? And in this peer group?' (Kuczaj 1998: 161).

Counter-transference

There are therapists who have written about understanding the experience of having learning disabilities by describing their counter-transference responses during and after sessions. In *Drawing on Difference* some art therapists have spoken frankly about their own feelings during and after sessions. Feeling 'stupid' and disempowered (Hallas and Lomas 1998: 52–53), inadequate and self doubting (Rees 1998: 240) are common counter-transference responses which can ultimately help us as therapists understand how clients with learning disabilities feel. Hallas and Lomas (1998) describe an art therapy group for people with learning disabilities. They state that the experience of learning disability was a central theme in the group, and that this was communicated in different ways. An argument often erupted between certain members which had the effect of making therapists feel 'useless' and unable to think. It was difficult to talk openly about learning disabilities.

Rees (1998) writes about the importance of exploring the counter-transference within the context of supervision. She speaks frankly about the 'tedium' one can feel in sessions, as being like 'a thick blanket which is thrown over the therapist preventing her from engaging with the client but also, at a more fundamental level, robbing her of her vitality and life force' (ibid.: 241). She acknowledges that this feeling can prevent the therapist from thinking about and addressing painful issues in therapy. She goes on to say that more crucially it is a feeling of 'suffocation or drowning – in short of dying' (ibid.). Rees wonders if this comes from an inner sense of being unwanted, of feeling that one shouldn't exist.

Thomas (2001), in her paper on working with institutional dynamics, talks about the 'apparent absence of feeling' (ibid.: 26) when working with staff teams who work with people with learning disabilities. She cites work she did with the staff of a small group home. She describes feelings of 'flatness and frustration' (ibid.: 27) when a staff member talked about trying to teach a resident with learning disabilities how to do up her own buttons. The resident was shown over and over, but 'wouldn't' learn how to do the task for herself. Thomas then experienced pressure from the staff, wanting her to make things better and come up with solutions, to take away from the 'depressed helplessness' (ibid.) they felt. What became apparent was that the success of the staff team depended greatly on what they could get their clients to achieve. Thomas helped the staff team to redefine their aims for their clients, having helped them to get in touch with their denied feelings.

Symington (1992) writes about denied feelings in relation to feelings of contempt for people with learning disabilities. In his workshops at the Tavistock Clinic he challenges students to think about their contempt and how this can be revealed through reactions to people with learning disabilities through feelings of guilt and pity. Symington says there is a learning disability enclave in each of us which is 'unbearable'. This can lead to contempt towards people damaged or less fortunate than ourselves (ibid.: 137). Contempt can lead to feelings of guilt and pity towards people with learning disabilities and this then stifles any development in them. Symington cites Clark (1933) who wrote about clients who immediately regress in therapy; if there is a 'thrust towards birth' (Symington 1992: 138) the therapist's task then is a very difficult one, as we are helping clients deal with an 'indescribable amount' of psychic 'pain'. Any development in therapy can be thwarted. He says a first step is the recognition of contempt, and thus the learning disability, in ourselves.

In summary, what each of these writers is saying is that if we deny the painful feelings in ourselves about learning disabilities and feelings associated with it, we are denying them in our clients, and creating barriers to them being truly listened to and understood.

The following is an account of art therapy sessions with a man called Patrick, with whom I worked for a two-year period. Out of necessity I have summarised the work and tried to pick out the relevant sessions which highlight the main issues and show significant changes as therapy progressed.

Patrick

Patrick is a Caucasian man with Down's syndrome. He was referred to art therapy as he had become withdrawn and was isolating himself following the death of a friend, a fellow resident, on holiday. Patrick and his friend had been with a group of residents on holiday together. Both his parents had died some years ago and, at the time of the referral, he was living in a large residential unit which was due to be closed within the next few months. Plans were being made for the residents to move into alternative accommodation.

The referral to the Community Team stated that Patrick had previously been very sociable and his interests included acting and watching videos, mostly pop, musicals and horror films.

The sessions

Patrick used many characters from popular culture in his sessions. He was particularly drawn to characters from horror films, such as Frankenstein, Dracula, the Werewolf and the Mummy from *The Curse of the Mummy*. Two of his favourite characters were the Phantom from the story *Phantom of the Opera* (Leroux 1909–1910), and King Kong. The Phantom first appeared in the second week of art therapy. He had just seen the stage production with his key worker, Amy.

At the beginning of the session he brought in the programme from the stage production. He kept pointing to the picture of the mask on the front of the programme and asked me to watch as he proceeded to sing in an operatic voice. He demonstrated the Phantom being shot, then made a drawing of a mask (Figure 2.1) in black pen.

Figure 2.1 Patrick: Mask 1.

I was not then familiar with the story of *Phantom of the Opera* and asked Patrick, 'Is it a sad story?' He said that it was. He made other drawings of various masks in the session. I asked him, 'Why does the Phantom wear a mask?' He told me it was 'to cover up a scar'. I said 'people sometimes use masks to hide something of themselves. When we wear masks other people cannot see how we are really feeling.' He asked me 'What do you mean?' I tried saying it another way. I wondered whether Patrick was hiding behind the mask as there were things about himself he wasn't sure he could reveal to me. He did not respond, but continued to draw.

Patrick continued to bring his *Phantom* programme into the session for weeks afterwards. In the next session, he insisted on cutting out a mask made the previous week, wanting my help with cutting out the eyes and mouth. Once finished, he held the mask to his face, pretending to be the Phantom. He got up from his seat and sang his version of 'Opera'. Some of the words were difficult to understand, but he sang the name 'Christine', the main female part, very loudly and clearly and with great passion. He then dramatically pulled the mask away from his face to reveal the 'scar'. I tried asking him about the story, 'Does the Phantom love Christine?' 'Does Christine love him?' As was often the case, Patrick ignored me and continued with his acting, so that I felt rather shut out by him. As I felt shut out, I reiterated what I had said the previous week about Patrick finding ways of hiding things about himself that he did not want people to see. He continued to ignore me.

Several weeks later, and the first session after a two-week break, Patrick began by drawing two shapes he said were 'the mask', which I understood to be the holes for the eyes (Figure 2.2).

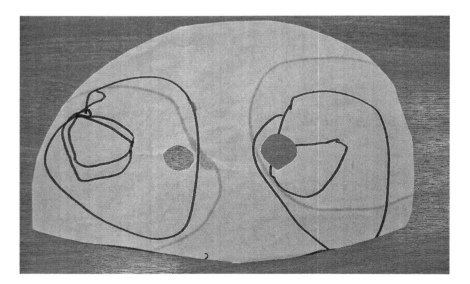

Figure 2.2 Patrick: Mask 2.

He told me that Amy was away at the moment and I acknowledged my break, and the fact that we had not seen each other for three weeks. He thumped his drawing lightly with his fist and then tapped his face, saying 'The Phantom of the Opera mask', then, 'has a scar'. At this stage in the therapy I associated the references to the scar as being about pain associated with loss. On reflection, I wonder if he was trying to get me to acknowledge his disability and I just wasn't getting it. With hindsight, had I made an interpretation early on and got stuck with it?

Throughout the following sessions Patrick continued to make masks and play with them, putting them to his face and then pulling them away to reveal his 'scar', saying 'Phantom takes off his mask and then he gets shot.' I commented on how the Phantom felt he had to keep the mask on, as if he would come to some harm if he took it off. It felt like he was not only expressing some aspects of himself through the use of the mask, but he seemed to need it as some form of protection. Was he, through the mask, saying something in relation to his disability and whether or not it could be possible to think about it? Could I bear it? It was only later that I realised the full significance of his use of the mask, my understanding aided by actually seeing the musical, to fully appreciate the story of the Phantom.

The Phantom, a powerful and elusive figure lurks in the basement of the Paris Opera House. He is the mentor of a young opera singer, Christine, whom he has taught to sing. She believes he is an angel that has been sent to her by her dead father. He is obsessed with her and they appear to share intense feelings for each other. She eventually rejects his love and chooses another.

In the sessions just before and after the move, Patrick's communication became more violent. He enacted violent horror films and stabbing women. There was much in his communication about sexuality and associated feelings of disappointment and anger. I felt personally attacked but found it difficult at that time to address these feelings. I focused on the loss of his home, asking him whether he felt sad. He said 'I am.'

I arrived at the residential unit for the last time and was astounded to find that in the days leading up to the move Patrick's bedroom had been moved to the room where we had been having the art therapy sessions. Many of his possessions were around him and items of furniture had been moved in. I tried to find out why this was so and was told that as it was a training flat, Patrick might be helped towards the move as he could experience being a little more independent. I felt very uneasy about the room that we had identified and established as our art therapy space being turned into Patrick's bedroom and wondered if he did too, especially given the sexual and violent images he had been presenting to me in previous sessions. Patrick drew (Plate 2.1) Dracula, with cape billowing out around his head, showing the red lining, baring teeth, with blood pouring from the mouth. Included in the image are a bat, the moon and two coffins. I felt that this image could reflect his violent yet helpless feelings. Blood drips from Dracula's and the bat's mouths, yet Dracula looks rather boyish and his teeth are crooked and blunt, as if they are about to fall out. The figure has no lower body and is therefore without genitalia. The coffins could represent the loss not only of his home but all the other losses, also possibly loss of 'normality'. I thought of Patrick the man, who seemed so much more like a boy.

Patrick said, 'Amy going.' He said that he missed his parents, pointing to a photograph he had of them. I acknowledged how painful it must be to have lost his mum and dad and now to be moving from his home and losing his key worker, Amy. (Some of the staff and other residents were moving with him but Amy was leaving to work elsewhere.) Patrick agreed to me looking after his pictures and I arranged for us to have future sessions at his new accommodation. A neutral office-type room was allocated to us. Patrick now had his own flat within a small complex of flats, with 24-hour staff support.

A few weeks after the move, Patrick brought a video of *King Kong* into the session. On the front cover was an image of King Kong holding the female victim as he towered over New York. The woman looked distressed and Patrick particularly wanted to draw my attention to her in the monster's clutches. I had seen the film years before, but had forgotten at this stage that King Kong was indeed the real victim in this story.

In the following session, he said 'watch' while he enacted King Kong, then the screaming woman and then the end of the film, when King Kong is shot. As he did this, he got very involved and I felt shut out and found the storyline difficult to follow. I attempted to make a connection between this story and that of *Phantom*, saying that, in both, the male characters are frightening because in different ways they are 'monsters'. In both stories the male characters are in love with a woman, but the women are scared. In both, the male characters are sad and desperate. In Patrick's version the Phantom gets killed. Although he scares everyone, King Kong is sad, as is the Phantom; neither can have the love of the woman.

Patrick continued to draw violent images. One of these is of a figure wearing a black mask holding a knife and a club. Patrick said that the man had killed a girl. He insisted that he bring down a book about horror films from his room. Although it is a book of images from films and therefore a potentially 'safe' way for Patrick to express his aggression, there was something about his use of the book and his behaviour which made me feel uncomfortable. I felt that I needed to say something about his preoccupation with violence against women, and I wondered if he thought about how this might make me feel. Patrick seemed to hear me. I said that I wondered if he felt very angry and frustrated and this was why he liked to see images of women getting hurt, again drawing a connection with the male characters in the films he liked. The male characters are powerful, but they are also very sad. I wondered if Patrick was aware of their being both frightening but also very sad.

In the sessions that followed, I felt as if Patrick had considered me and what I'd said in relation to the violent imagery and was starting to acknowledge me as a separate person, and there was more interaction between us. He talked about his old residential home for the first time then said that he would like to draw me. I said that he might need to look at me in order to be able to draw me. He then, at my suggestion, drew a picture of himself and we looked at our differences. I acknowledged the obvious difference, that he was a man and I was a woman. He said that he was a 'boy'. I wondered about his calling himself a boy and asked about the expression on the face of the 'boy'. He said he looked 'sad'.

In the next session Patrick enacted a werewolf being shot by a boy. We looked back at the picture made of him and me the previous week. I noted that he was not wearing a mask in the picture. He wanted to make the picture of me into a mask by cutting it out and said that my face looked ugly, then that it looked sad. He said that his face looked sad. I asked, 'What could be making your face sad?' He said the name of his last home 'closing'.

Patrick talked of going to see *Phantom* with Amy and then looked at himself in the mirror. He said 'scar face'. I wondered if Patrick felt a bit like the Phantom because he had a disability too. He said 'yes'. This was the first time that I directly acknowledged his having a learning disability. This seemed to lead us in subsequent sessions to think more about the issue of maturation and Patrick seemed to be more accepting of his being a man, rather than a boy. This theme continued through the character of Wolfman when he talked of *Wolfman* getting more and more hairy and how he was 'changing'.

During this period he made mask pictures which, rather than hide, actually reveal the scar (Plate 2.2). The 'mask' turned on its side has one eye emphasised and there is a blackened area above it, which could be a scar.

I found it was very difficult to start addressing the end of therapy with Patrick because of the numerous losses Patrick had recently experienced. He was certainly less withdrawn and he had been able to explore some very pertinent issues in the sessions, to do with being learning disabled, loss and sexuality. Having moved into a new flat, he was more involved in doing things for himself and was becoming more independent. With all the difficult changes that had gone on in his life, I felt there had been some positive ones. Through our growing relationship, I felt he was now seeing me more as a separate person and communication had become more two-way and it was because of this that we could acknowledge our differences and his having a learning disability.

Discussion

As stated in the theory section, over-protection can be damaging to healthy development. Patrick has Down's syndrome which would have been seen at his birth. His use of the Phantom and the mask is a very explicit communication about his own marked disability. Patrick felt more like a boy and struggled to accept that he was a man. However, through much of the communication about the Werewolf, 'changing', i.e. becoming more hairy, it seems there was some maturation during the course of therapy. This happened when I talked directly about Patrick's disability.

Having had an opportunity to reflect on the art therapy sessions with Patrick, I realise that I continued to ignore his communication (through the use of the phantom mask) about his disability. I talked about it directly a long time into therapy, when Patrick was looking at his reflection in the mirror and said 'scar face'.

It was such a direct communication that I couldn't continue to ignore it. At this stage in therapy, we had developed a relationship and had already done a lot of work together, focusing mainly on the closure and loss of his former home. Seeing *Phantom of the Opera* myself some time into therapy, and getting to know the story, helped me to understand that much of his communication was about his having a disability.

Whilst he used the stories he was familiar with and which spoke to him in very profound ways, Patrick identified with and immersed himself in the characters so much that he actually felt he was the character. At times I felt this was defensive and I wonder if there was some (albeit unconscious) attempt at blocking my thinking. On the many occasions when I attempted to talk about painful issues, he seemed not to hear and I felt pushed away. It was through addressing our relationship more directly that some attention was paid to our gender differences and he referred to himself being a boy, rather than a man. This led to his exploration of our differences in terms of disability, saying first that he wanted to turn the drawing of my face into a mask, then that it looked ugly, then that it looked sad. He went on to think about his own sadness and, looking in the mirror, said 'scar face'. This communication between us is interesting if we consider the early relationship between caregiver and infant (Sinason 1992). It is as if he was noticing the caregiver's look of disappointment and sadness and then realised why I (as 'caregiver') seemed sad when he went to the mirror and saw the reflection of himself.

It is interesting that Patrick's interpretation of the story of the Phantom was that he became scarred through an accident, an explosion, rather than a congenital condition. It is possible that, because Patrick looks obviously learning disabled, he needed to see the story of the Phantom in this way, as he understood his disability to be caused by an 'accident'. Patrick often referred to the 'scar' on his own face, pointing to the marked eczema around his eyes. However, he could have also have been referring to his characteristically shaped eyes, these being one of the indicators of his having Down's syndrome.

Transference

Patrick's transference towards me was also being explored through his use of the Phantom and King Kong characters particularly. Both characters are longing for the woman, and go to great lengths to win her love, but in the process become frightening and the women are scared, as I was beginning to be at times in the sessions. The stories are very sad and tragic, being about unrequited love.

In her book about erotic transference, Schaverien (1995) says that a significant woman in a man's life can be felt to be very powerful, the mother being all important to the child. Ambivalent feelings can arise because of his dependence on her. This ambivalence can also be experienced in the therapeutic relationship. I would suggest that this ambivalence is further complicated in people with learning disabilities, who are often more dependent on others for their very survival. It is possible that in the transference Patrick sometimes saw me as a mother and sometimes a potential partner whom he simultaneously desired, envied and hated. Schaverien says that the therapist must not collude with the denigration of women but 'confront empathically' (citing Woods 1976). In our sessions, the increasing violence was addressed and consciously thought about and, partly because of this, he started to see me as a separate person.

The use of iconic images from popular culture in art therapy

Monsters can be used to express feelings about developing sexuality (Goldberg 1991). Also Twitchell (1985) writes about the monster in horror films expressing adolescent anxiety about sexuality and the fear of it. Patrick used the Werewolf in very obvious ways to either deny or show me his being a man, by talking about the Werewolf 'changing'. The monster appeared at the time when he was starting to be more separate from me and this was also the time when he had moved to his flat and was starting to lead a slightly more independent life.

I have become very interested in the use of popular culture in art therapy sessions, since noticing its use by many clients with learning disabilities (Caven 2005). The debate continues about the negative influence of TV and film on children and young people. In the case I have described, I would suggest that Patrick was drawn to particular productions and characters as they spoke to him in quite profound ways. It is not just the story or character which was of importance, but how they were used with me in the art therapy sessions. Patrick's use of popular iconic imagery was often very intense and for a long period of time he would be completely immersed in the characters and stories of his fantasies.

Wood (1999) cites Richards' (1994) work when considering class issues and the backgrounds of many of our clients, saying that, to a lot of our clients from working-class backgrounds, this form of media is more familiar than others. Richards argues that popular culture can be profound. We find pleasure in feeling reassured by the social nature of much popular cultural activity: 'Participation in popular culture reaffirms the containing social matrix of which we are a part, to which we belong and which belongs to us' (ibid.: 7).

It is interesting, in view of this, to consider people with learning disabilities who can often feel different and outside the 'norm'. As stated earlier, Kuczaj discusses themes of 'similarity and difference' saying these are common threads amongst people with learning disabilities in art therapy sessions. Through the shared knowledge and common language of film, TV and popular music, genres very familiar to learning disabled and non-learning disabled alike, the learning disabled can explore difference through popular stories and characters in art therapy (Caven 2005).

The stories of the *Phantom of the Opera* and *King Kong* are similar. Wells (2000) writes about the horror genre, saying these films deal with 'social alienation' (ibid.: 6): the monsters threaten the status quo. There is a connection here with what Sinason (1992) and Bicknell (1983: 172) say about the learning disabled infant being, in a sense, a threat to the status quo of the family. The grieving parents are left to cope with the loss of the 'perfect child' (ibid.: 168; Marvin and Piñata 1996) and their guilt associated with this. Patrick was dealing with the difficult issue of being perceived as an outsider, because of having learning disabilities. Many of today's stories depicted on our television screens, reflect society's preoccupations and thus the inner psyche of us as individuals. According to Zizek (2006) if something becomes too much we fictionalise it. Patrick discovered that his own story was mirrored in that of the Phantom and other characters brought into art therapy. Interestingly, it is through having this opportunity to reflect that I realise it was through seeing the stage production myself that I understood much more about what Patrick was trying to tell me. It is possible that seeing and gaining an understanding of the story of the Phantom gave me permission to address Patrick's disability directly.

I would suggest that by taking popular iconic imagery seriously, when used by clients in art therapy sessions, we are accepting them, as popular culture is very accessible and an obvious choice of visual media for many people. We can make full use of what people bring into art therapy and because of the nature of art therapy and the largely psychotherapeutic model used, we have the opportunity to explore the personal meaning behind the stories and characters (Caven 2005). The painful issue of having a learning disability can be explored through this medium in a way that feels bearable, as it is shared between the learning disabled and non-learning disabled alike.

I find that it is often hard to address the learning disability but we can find ways of doing so in art therapy sessions by listening to and using what is brought into the sessions.

The learning disability in us all

Being non-learning disabled it is hard to completely imagine what it must be like to have a learning disability. Thomas (2001) and Symington (1992) say that as therapists we need to acknowledge our learning disability if we are to enable people with learning disabilities to move forward. In my work as an art therapist I have often felt devalued. I found it helpful to read about Hallas and Lomas's (1998) accounts of feeling 'useless' and Rees's counter-transference responses (1998), as I recognise these in myself when in art therapy sessions with people with learning disabilities. When I began work with Patrick I had little experience of working with people with learning disabilities, and feelings of not being a particularly good art therapist were overwhelming at times. I liken this feeling of inadequacy to being alone in a foreign country where we are unfamiliar with the language and customs. Most of us feel bewildered, lost and inadequate in alien surroundings; and in certain situations where we are rendered 'stupid'. This can feel very frustrating at best and at times frightening and debilitating. If I can feel disabled in certain situations some of the time, then I can only try to imagine what it must feel like for a lot of people with learning disabilities in many situations most of the time.

References

Barnett, D., Clements, M., Kaplan-Estrin, M. and Fialka, J. 2003. 'Building New Dreams: Supporting Parents' Adaptation to their Child with Special Needs'. *Infants and Young Children* 18(4): 295–307.

Bicknell, J. 1983. 'The Psychopathology of Handicap'. *British Journal of Medical Psychology* 56: 167–178.

Bion, W. 1959. 'Attacks on Linking'. *International Journal of Psychoanalysis* 40.

Bion, W. 1967. *Second Thoughts.* New York: Jason Aronson.

Bowlby, J. 1969. *Attachment and Loss: Attachment Vol. 1: Loss.* London: The Hogarth Press and The Institute of Psycho-Analysis.

Bowlby, J. 1980. *Attachment and Loss: Loss Vol. 3: Loss.* London: The Hogarth Press and The Institute of Psycho-Analysis.

Caven, J. 2005. A Case Study Based Research Project Which Explores the Use of Popular Iconic Imagery in the Artwork of People with Learning Disabilities in Art Therapy Sessions. Unpublished Masters in Research in Art Psychotherapy (PACE), Goldsmiths College, University of London.

Clark, P. 1933. *The Nature and Treatment of Amentia.* London: Bailliere, Tindall and Cox.

Cooper, Merian C. and Shoedsack, Ernest B. (dirs). 1933. *King Kong* [film]. USA.

Fiennes, S. (dir.). 2006. *The Pervert's Guide to the Cinema* [DVD]. A Lone Star Production, Mischief Films, Amoeba Film Production. Scripted and presented by Slavoj Zizek.

Goldberg, D. 1991. *From Monsters to Moons, Universal and Culturally Specific Symbols in Psychotherapy.* Inscape. The British Association of Art Therapists.

Hallas, P. and Lomas, H. 1998. 'It's a Mystery: Accounts of an Art Therapy Group for People with Learning Disabilities'. In Rees, M. (ed.) *Drawing on Difference: Art Therapy with People who have Learning Difficulties.* London and New York: Routledge.

Julian, Rupert (dir.). 1925. *The Phantom of the Opera* [film]. USA.

Kubler-Ross, E. 1970. *On Death and Dying.* London: Tavistock Publications.

Kuczaj, E. 1998. 'Learning to Say "Goodbye": Loss and Bereavement in Learning Difficulties and the Role of Art Therapy'. In Rees, M. (ed.) *Drawing on Difference: Art Therapy with People who have Learning Difficulties.* London and New York: Routledge.

Leroux, G. (1909–1910). *Le Fantome de l'Opera.* From the magazine *Le Gaulois.* Paris.

Lloyd Webber, A. (comp.). Started 1986. *The Phantom of the Opera* [musical]. Her Majesty's Theatre, London.

Marvin, R. S. and Piñata, R. C. 1996. 'Mothers' Reactions to their Child's Diagnosis: Relations with Security of Attachment'. *Journal of Clinical Psychology* 25(4): 436–445.

Rees, M. 1998. 'Clinical Supervision in Art Therapy'. In Rees, M. (ed.) *Drawing on Difference: Art Therapy with People who have Learning Difficulties.* Routledge.

Richards, B. 1994. *Disciplines of Delight: The Psychoanalysis of Popular Culture.* London: Free Association Books.

Schaverien, J. 1995. *Desire and the Female Therapist: Engendered Gazes in Psychotherapy Art Therapy.* London: Brunner and Routledge.

Schumacher, J. (dir.). 2004. Andrew Lloyd-Webber's *Phantom of the Opera* [film]. London.

Sinason, V. 1992. *Mental Handicap and the Human Condition: New Approaches from the Tavistock.* London: Free Association Books.

Symington, N. 1992. 'Countertransference with Mentally Handicapped Clients'. In Waitman, A. and Conboy-Hill, S. (eds) *Psychotherapy and Mental handicap.* London: Sage Publications.

Szivos, S. and Griffiths, E. 1992. 'Coming to Terms with Learning Difficulties: The Effects of Groupwork and Group Processes on Stigmatised Identity in Psychotherapy and Mental Handicap'. In Waitman, A. and Conboy-Hill, S. (eds) *Psychotherapy and Mental Handicap*. London: Sage Publications.

Thomas, B. 2001. '"I've Taught you Once Already": Forgetting the Disability in Learning Disability'. *Clinical Psychology Forum* 148.

Twitchell, J. B. 1985. *Dreadful Pleasures: An Anatomy of Modern Horror.* Oxford/New York: Oxford University Press.

Wells, P. 2000. *The Horror Genre: From Beezlebub to Blair Witch.* Short Cuts. London: Wallflower.

Winnicott, D. W. 1971. *Playing and Reality.* London: Penguin.

Wood, C. 1999. 'Class Issues in Art Therapy'. In Campbell, J., Liebmann, M., Brooks, F., Jones, J. and Ward, C. (eds) *Art Therapy, Race and Culture.* London and Philadelphia: Jessica Kingsley Publishers.

Woods, S. M. 1976. 'Some Dynamics of Male Chauvinism'. *Archives of General Psychiatry* 33: 63–65.

Part II

Loss

Bereavement and learning disabilities

A theoretical overview

Kim Dee

The following two chapters are focused on the theme of loss which is a pervasive theme in art therapy with people with learning disabilities. As an introduction to the two case examples, I give a brief overview of literature and theory on bereavement, loss and learning disabilities.

Before the late 1970s, the emotional development of people with learning disabilities was rarely considered separately from their intellectual development, and there was an assumption that loss and grief were not experienced in the same way as in the general population (Oswin 1991). Early research (Emerson 1977) found that both staff and family frequently did not make a link between changes in behaviour of people with learning disabilities and their recent experiences of bereavement. Hollins and Esterhuyzen (1997) found that people with learning disabilities who had not attended a parent's funeral were more likely to develop complex grief reactions and that their difficulties were unlikely to be recognised as being connected to their experience of loss.

It was also assumed that people with learning disabilities did not have the cognitive capacity to address emotional difficulties through psychological therapies (Blackman 2003). Historically, medication and behaviour modification programmes have been considered as the first treatment options (Hollins and Esterhuyzen 1997). Valerie Sinason (1992) and other members of the Tavistock Clinic, London, initiated some of the first psychotherapeutic work with people with learning disabilities and Conboy-Hill (1992) in particular highlighted the need for psychotherapeutic input to assist people with learning disabilities in addressing bereavement. In the first art therapy book on working with people with learning disabilities, *Drawing on Difference*, a chapter was devoted to working with loss (Kuczaj 1998). The important role of arts psychotherapists in helping people with learning disabilities deal with loss is also increasingly recognised in literature outside the art therapy field (see Blackman 2003 and Grey 2010).

Oswin's ground-breaking book, *Am I allowed to Cry?* (1991), gave numerous case examples of grief expressed by people with learning disabilities and made the point that this grief is akin to that experienced by the non-learning disabled population. However, she also highlighted that grief can be more complex for people with learning disabilities and that there are a number of factors which can contribute to this including:

- Loss of normal opportunities throughout life such as: sexual relationships, children and full employment.
- Difficult/damaged attachments with parents in early childhood (see Chapter 6).
- Limited life experience, including possibly not having had the opportunity to rehearse or explore death in childhood play.
- Limited verbal communication.
- Other people's misattribution of behaviours associated with the expression of grief to disability or psychiatric illness.
- People with learning disabilities may have limited ability to understand and process events intellectually, but this does not mean that profound grief is not experienced on an emotional level.
- Dependency on carers, particularly parents, into adulthood and the common experience of losing a home and being moved to a new environment at the same time as the loss of a primary carer.
- Non-attendance at funerals and being expected to carry on as normal, e.g. attending the day centre whilst other family members have time off work for bereavement. Sometimes people find themselves placed in an unfamiliar respite facility to give the family a break during preparations for a funeral.
- The person who died may have been their only confidante – the one who understood and met their needs, leaving the bereaved person isolated and lonely.

Bereavement is not an illness but a normal, if difficult, life experience which most of us will have to face at some point in our lives. It should not be assumed that people need immediate specialist support or medical intervention. People with learning disabilities are sometimes automatically referred for therapy following bereavement rather than just being allowed to adjust to their loss in their own way. Many people with learning disabilities are supported at home and at day centres by support staff who, though often unqualified, may have years of experience of providing care. As frontline staff they can play a vital role in supporting bereaved people with learning disabilities and identifying when they are having problems following bereavement and require extra input. Sympathetic acknowledgement of the loss of a loved one from someone they already know can go a long way in helping a bereaved person to feel less alone at this time. Support staff can also get involved in visiting graves with the person or marking anniversaries in other ways and this can help with the process of grieving.

Bereavement theory

Bowlby's attachment theory characterised bereavement as a type of separation anxiety with its roots in the primary attachment to the mother. He believed that an individual who did not experience a 'secure' primary attachment as a child was more likely to have problems resolving grief in later life due to the absence of a strong, internalised sense of security (Bowlby 1979). This theory has particular relevance to people with learning disabilities who have often experienced disrupted early attachments for various reasons including:

- Early separation from the mother for long periods for medical intervention.
- Parents may have had difficulty accepting the child and experienced a form of grief at the loss of the hoped for 'perfect' child (Sinason 1992) and/or felt shame and embarrassment in their community, which the child will have perceived at some level.
- Children with learning disabilities may have been institutionalised at an early age, involving a traumatic separation from their parents (this is less common now but is still the experience of many people with learning disabilities over 30 years of age).
- Parents may have an overly anxious attachment to a child due to perceptions of them as ill rather than disabled and in need of constant protection and monitoring.

Early psychotherapeutic theory on bereavement emphasised the need to relinquish the lost loved one, in order to be able to move on in life and form new relationships. There is now growing understanding and appreciation of the benefits of assisting people in remembering and valuing the relationship they had with a deceased loved one (Klass *et al.* 1996). In Chapter 3, I illustrate the positive outcomes of helping someone to do this rather than avoiding the subject for fear of upsetting them.

A number of theorists such as Worden (2001) have identified phases or stages in grief. These phases can be helpful in understanding the overwhelming emotions which a bereaved person can experience. They are also beneficial in reassuring people that it is normal to feel disorientated, despairing and angry and so on when a loved one dies. However, grieving is not a neat orderly process and can be particularly difficult and lengthy when a person has learning disabilities. The two case examples which follow illustrate this.

In therapeutic work related to loss with people with learning disabilities it is also important to reflect on:

- Your own experiences of loss, in particular unresolved feelings.
- Religious and culturally specific ceremonies, traditions and attitudes towards death, dying and bereavement.
- Society's attitude towards people with learning disabilities (in particular the concept of society's 'death wish' towards people with learning disabilities) (Sinason 1992).

Chapter 3

Shaping loss

Kim Dee

Introduction

'Nice to see you, to see you, nice!' Bruce Forsyth and Tommy Cooper imper-sonations were not the first thing that I would have predicted when contemplating bereavement work with a person referred to me for art therapy. I imagined something altogether more solemn. In the event, humour sat cheek by jowl with profound sadness and anger in Paul's art therapy sessions.

In this chapter I explore:

- The use of art materials in re-enacting experiences of loss including mourning rituals.
- How art therapy enables people with learning disabilities, and limited verbal communication, to address their loss and set the pace of therapy, without the pressure for verbal exchange.
- Identification and exploration of ambiguous/ambivalent feelings in relation to the deceased.
- The importance of working with the person's network and with other profes-sionals to meet the person's needs.
- Use of educational materials in therapy.

Referral and assessment – a systemic perspective

It is important to extend horizons beyond the therapy room and borrow from systemic therapy in engaging with all the 'systems' that a person in therapy is part of, including home and day placements. Paul did not refer himself to therapy and, in my experience, it is still unusual for people with learning disabilities to self-refer for services. Often the reason given for referrals I receive is defined more in terms of difficulties dealing with behaviour rather than concern for the person's emotional well-being. Paul was threatened with expulsion from the day centre and relations and communication had broken down between his family and day centre staff. Paul had shown signs of distress for two years after his father died and, despite him repeatedly drawing an image of his father and a 'churchyard', Paul was not referred to psychological therapies until day centre staff found his behaviour increasingly unmanageable.

People can come across quite differently in different environments. Looking at the whole picture, liaising with people who play a big part in Paul's life was crucial for me to gain insight into his situation and essential to Paul attending therapy.

I am a part of a community multidisciplinary team, which includes psychiatrists, psychologists, speech therapists and occupational therapists. Our team approach is always to have the perspective of more than one discipline in initial assessments and formulation. Reviews and case feedback are also carried out in a multidisciplinary forum. Part of the assessment process is to establish the person's consent to engage in therapy and, if possible, what they hope to gain from it.

Day centre visit

Paul was referred to art therapy by his day centre key worker who was concerned about an increase over the past couple of years in behaviours which staff found challenging such as spitting, self-isolation, angry outbursts and some physical aggression towards other people attending the day centre. Paul had repeatedly drawn an image which he identified as his father and 'a churchyard' or 'graveyard' (Plate 3.1). He also frequently pointed towards the ceiling and said 'Dad' whilst looking upset. As it was a first referral to the multidisciplinary team, I carried out an initial assessment jointly with a team psychologist.

We first met Paul at his day centre with his key worker and later at home with family members. His key worker had tried various ways of addressing Paul's 'deteriorating behaviour' without any success and was worried that he may have to be excluded from the centre. Staff had not formally discussed with Paul the impact of his father's death (two years before) on him nor acknowledged what had happened in any significant way. This was because they had some anxiety about how Paul's family would respond if they did, partly due to strained relations.

Paul seemed shy and had a pronounced stutter. He answered our questions, but clearly needed extra time to think as there was a long delay in his answers and sometimes he appeared to be answering previous questions. However, he nodded vigorously when we talked about his father and pointed at his drawings and up to the ceiling, saying 'Dad'. Paul was in his late thirties but appeared younger. He was small and there was something boyish about his appearance and manner. His expression was lively and curious – as if he was very interested in us.

His key worker said that he was amongst the youngest of the people at the day centre and tended to be treated as a 'youngster' or 'naughty boy' by them (key worker's words). Paul had been diagnosed as having Down's syndrome as a child but had few of the distinguishing physical features and I would not have recognised this without being informed. He spent a lot of time at the day centre on his own, isolating himself in places where he seemed to feel safer and sometimes spitting or waving around a plastic baseball bat if other people at the day centre came close.

Home visit

Paul was noticeably more relaxed in his home environment but his mother seemed very guarded about us getting involved. He is part of a loving, close-knit, working-class family. He had always lived at home with his parents and was brought up alongside his older sister, although they had attended different schools. Paul had gone to the local special needs school.

Paul's mother felt that he had been negatively labelled by the day centre and was often blamed for things, which, she believed, arose from others who may have been bullying him. His family seemed angry with the day centre and felt that little had been done by services and professionals to help Paul. They were of the opinion that it was too late to do anything now.

His mother said she was not aware that Paul was preoccupied with the death of his father and she had not been told about the drawings which he had been making at the day centre and which Paul always named as 'Dad and a churchyard'. To some extent she seemed to be in denial about this as she later acknowledged that Paul was confused about his father's death and that he sometimes asked when Dad was coming back. Paul had also been spitting on the floor more at home since his father's death and following his mother around. She said she was nervous about the death being brought up in front of Paul, for fear it would upset him.

His father's illness had been quite sudden and Paul did not visit him in hospital or see him seriously unwell. In addition, he had not attended the funeral as his family were worried that it would upset and confuse him and thought he might disrupt the service. According to Paul's sister, he saw his father's coffin in the funeral hearse but his mum decided it would be best for him not to come into the church so he did not witness the ceremony or burial. He sat outside the church in a car with a relative until the funeral service and burial were over. Paul's mum acknowledged that the family still viewed him as a child and sought to protect him from difficult things. In the subsequent two years he had not visited the grave.

She said that when Paul asked about his father, she pointed upwards and said that he was 'up there now' (meaning in heaven) and at rest. The family were not religious and it is unlikely that Paul had a concept of heaven or of an afterlife. Paul occasionally asked when his dad was coming back after his mum gave her reply. She said that Paul had tended to 'take more notice' of what his dad said than of what she said and that he had 'really looked up to him'.

Outcome of assessment and actions

Paul's eagerness to show the picture of his dad and the churchyard and to explain that he was 'sad' indicated that he was interested in having a space to explore his feelings about the loss of his father. I usually offer people who have been referred to me at least four art therapy assessment sessions to help them get a better grasp of what art therapy involves, before agreeing a therapeutic contract with them.

Paul's mother was sceptical about art therapy input, worrying that it would upset him further about his father's death. I sought to reassure her, pointing out that Paul was already upset about his father and needed help to address his feelings. She initially remained unconvinced but did not oppose him attending art therapy.

I was concerned that, as well as needing therapeutic input, Paul also needed some factual understanding of the concept of death and of what had actually happened to his father after he went into hospital. I discussed this with the team psychologist and we agreed that it was best to try and address this within the therapy sessions, as it naturally arose.

The value of systemic thinking extends beyond the assessment process. Deciding on the best way to involve people from the client's network in therapeutic work is also vital. In Paul's case a team psychologist worked alongside me in addressing issues with day centre staff and Paul's family. The psychologist worked with the network in generating ideas about how Paul's life could be improved, such as changes to his activity programme at the day centre.

Early sessions

Paul attended art therapy for a year. I was struck by how comfortable he seemed in the small art therapy room, right from the first session. Paul's family and day centre staff had said that he found change difficult and I had anticipated that Paul would take time to adjust to a new place, away from the day centre. However, he showed no signs of not wanting to be in the room and immediately made a beeline for the art materials. It may have helped that we had previously met in two familiar environments and that we had already talked about the referral being connected to the loss of his father.

Use of modelling material

In the first session Paul made an object from modelling material. He handed it to me with a heavy sigh, saying 'Dad'. I asked if he missed his dad and again he sighed with his whole body and put his hand to his forehead, saying 'yes'.

Paul had repeatedly drawn an image at the day centre before he attended art therapy (Plate 3.1) but it was striking that when offered a greater range of materials he immediately chose to use modelling material in therapy. The three-dimensional, tactile nature of the material seemed to help him connect in a more real, vital way with the physical loss of his father.

Imagining and recreating his father seemed necessary for Paul to begin to grasp what had actually happened to him. It was very moving to watch Paul handle the modelling material tenderly, reminding me of a parent carefully handling a baby in the bath. I later found out from his sister that, although Paul's father was not generally involved in his care, he had assisted Paul with bathing as an adult. His treatment of the modelling material made me think about the art objects he created as his father's body or coffin and tangibly brought his physical presence into the session.

Paul went on to draw the familiar image of 'Dad and churchyard' (Plate 3.1). This image is stark and graphic. There was a lack of connection between the elements of the picture; the face was quite separate from the parallel lines, sitting unhappily next to them. He pointed at the face in the picture and said 'sad'. I asked if he worried about his dad in the churchyard and he nodded. I then asked if he knew what had happened to his dad and, after a pause, he sighed, hung his head and said 'buried'. I asked him what happens when someone is buried. He looked at me directly and very clearly and forcefully said 'I don't know, what happens?' and then emphatically 'tell me!' There was a tinge of anger and sarcasm in the way he said this as if he had asked before and not got an answer. Awkwardly, I tried to explain what happens when someone dies and is buried. My words felt clumsy and difficult and I wondered if I might scare him more with my description, but he listened intently, sometimes nodding. At the end of the session Paul said he would like to pay a visit to the churchyard, and he agreed to me sharing this with his family and key worker.

Almost immediately, Paul seemed to embrace the art therapy room as a containing space where he could keep important things. At the end of the session Paul put his sculpted object onto a shelf in the cupboard, and his drawing into the folder and shut the cupboard doors.

Using educational resources within therapy

It is vital to take into account the person's learning disability in therapeutic work and consider how this may have contributed to their emotional difficulties. In Paul's case the use of picture books within the therapy sessions helped address his understanding of illness and death as it naturally arose in conjunction with his feelings.

I brought some picture books, specifically aimed at people with learning disabilities, on the topics of terminal illness, death and grieving into the therapy sessions. These included *When Dad Died* (Hollins and Sireling 2004) and a Mencap leaflet which included images of coffins, graves and churches. I did not direct Paul to look at them, but left them within his view to pick up if he wished. He asked me to read him *When Dad Died* (ibid.) and he renamed the family members in the book so that they matched his own, including his two nieces. Paul pointed at the dad in the book and at his own drawing of 'Dad', holding his head in his hands and looking sad as he gazed at the images.

In our third session Paul looked at images of coffins and wanted to know how the body fitted in. I made a rectangular box and put a strip of clay inside it and a lid on top. Paul closed and opened the lid several times and then pushed it down firmly, sealing it round the edges. He then added two lumps of clay to either end and fitted it carefully over the photo of the coffin in the booklet. He said 'Dad' pointing at the object. Paul looked upset, sighing heavily, and hid his face with his hand. I said I thought that he might be upset and that it must be difficult thinking about his dad like this; he nodded with his face covered. I wondered out loud if people had not realized how much Paul missed his dad and how upsetting it was to lose him in this way. We also talked more about what had actually happened to his father and about his burial; Paul was particularly concerned about his dad not being able to breathe in the coffin. To some extent, it felt brutal talking in this way. We are so used to using euphemism in relation to death, referring to people 'passing away' that trying to explain it in a straightforward way can feel uncomfortable. However, it also felt necessary to do so and Paul showed a keen interest and asked many questions.

Paul always used art materials in the sessions, particularly modelling material, but he also usually spent time looking at the books. He pointed at characters, named them and explained pictures to me. Paul's concentration and attention was remarkable during these times, as if he could not get enough of the story. A couple of times he took a book away without asking and I had to ask staff at the day centre to retrieve it. I wondered about the book as a transitional object from the sessions which he could hang on to. I gently raised the issue of taking the book with him and suggested he may have wanted to hold onto something good or comforting from the session.

The books helped Paul piece together a narrative for the loss of his father, shown in his renaming of the characters in one book. They also assisted him in reflecting on his bereavement and he used the images in the books to identify and communicate feelings, such as pointing at the picture of a distraught person and then pointing at himself and making a sad face. Paul incorporated images from the books directly into his art therapy process, such as when he placed a coffin shaped box over the photo of a coffin in a leaflet.

Re-enactment of mourning ceremonies within therapy

In the fourth session, Paul attempted to make a box out of synthetic modelling material but was frustrated by the pieces not sticking together. I suggested using clay and he took this up, but pulled an exaggerated face of disgust in reaction to the feel of the wet clay. The thought of bodies being buried in clay soil came into my mind and then the idea of bodies returning to 'clay' in death. This chilling thought was quickly displaced by Paul catching my eye and giggling about the mess on his hands whilst pulling a pantomime upset expression. The giggling continued for a while, with Paul repeatedly pointing at me with clay covered fingers and laughing. Then a wary look came across his face, I asked if he was OK and forcefully, he said, 'No', and pointed at his drawing of Dad. It seemed as though he was feeling guilty for having a moment of fun.

In a later session he again initially responded to the clay as if it was dirty, like faecal matter, but continued to work with it and eventually handed the object to me, saying 'I love you.' I was struck by the apparent disjunction between his expressed sentiment and the object as excrement. His objects often seemed to

Figure 3.1 Paul: Model 2.

contain dual qualities of tenderness and revulsion which reflected the difficult emotions and images he had about the loss of his father. The idea of his father's dead body was frightening but he could also make a box as a safe place to care for him and keep him.

Paul repeatedly acted out the process and ceremony of burial and grieving in the art therapy sessions, using modelling material to make box-like shapes.

After handing the box/coffins to me he would often look sad, shielding his face and sometimes crying. Noelle Blackman (2004) comments on the importance of ceremonies in the process of bereavement and even suggests creating an alternative ceremony for people who have not had the opportunity to attend funerals of a loved one. Re-enactment of the burial was part of Paul's process of mourning in the sessions and my role in witnessing and acknowledging his grief was crucial to this. The use of tactile modelling material added to the process of re-enactment, with the sense that he was really *shaping his loss* in a concrete way. Handling and looking together at these three-dimensional objects also contributed to the sense of his grief being held in the therapy – a very different experience from shared looking at a picture on a flat surface (Damarell 2007).

Middle sessions

Mimicking and counter-transference

There was often a point in the sessions when Paul became tearful and put his hands over his face while crying. Sometimes I spoke quietly about the pain of the loss of his father and how he may have felt that the people around him were not aware of his sadness. On one occasion I noticed that Paul was pausing between bouts of crying and peeping out at me between his fingers, smiling broadly, and I commented on what he was doing. He dropped his hands and laughed. He then leant forward on the table resting one hand on his chin, looking very serious and nodded in a concerned way and afterwards fell about laughing. I realised Paul was imitating me and my immediate feelings were of embarrassment, self-consciousness and a feeling of being somewhat ridiculous. In the counter-transference I also felt a moment of anger and affront with him. I felt Paul was mocking me and briefly doubted if any of his apparent sadness had been real and even if he had a learning disability. In that instant, I felt as though Paul had been playing games with me.

At the same time, I was impressed by Paul's accurate impersonation and I saw with clarity that as well as me observing him, he was studying me. It was as if we switched places for a moment and it was a most disconcerting feeling; much came out of this through further reflection and in supervision as the therapy progressed. Just before I noticed Paul peeping through his fingers I realised I had been feeling rather stuck in this repeated pattern in the session: acting out the burial and crying. In other words I felt as though I was just going through the motions in acknowledging Paul's grief and that this was apparent to him on a non-verbal level. Perhaps he had caught me out being partially insincere and bored. I also remembered his key worker telling me that other, older people attending his day centre viewed him as 'naughty' and found his behaviour annoying and upsetting.

I wondered if Paul was a bit of a tease and imitated staff and other people attending the day centre; this was confirmed when I spoke to his key worker at a later date. Clinical supervision gave me the opportunity to consider Paul's behaviour in a non-judgemental way and reflect on what might lie behind it, rather than staying within the painful counter-transference feelings which were initially evoked.

Observation skills and understanding others

Further reflection on what had happened made me think about Paul's need to observe and imitate others. Paul had word-finding difficulties and took a long time to process and respond to what was said to him. He had clearly developed other strategies in understanding and communicating with people, including closely observing mannerisms and facial expression. I realised from this particular moment in therapy that Paul was a keen observer of people and was likely to have picked up on the stress and grief of his family during his father's illness and subsequent death. His mum said she had avoided talking about what was going on in his presence as she felt it might upset him, so Paul had needed to rely on what was being communicated non-verbally through expression and posture. It is possible he had observed family members crying, looking upset, serious and even angry. They were likely to have been very preoccupied and busy and Paul may have experienced family members stopping talking when he came in the room and looking uncomfortable with him. I wondered if Paul had felt that he had done something wrong and felt excluded from his close-knit family at this time. Of course, during the funeral, he was literally excluded.

His habit of covering his face in therapy while he was crying suggested to me that he had learnt that crying was in some way shameful and unmanly, but it also made me think about his acute awareness of other people's facial expressions. Hiding his face meant that he could not be imitated, that the true strength of his feelings was not exposed and therefore could not be mocked.

Emergence of more complex and ambiguous feelings

In a later session, whilst working on a box-like construction using strips of coloured synthetic material (Plate 3.2), Paul suddenly started laughing almost uncontrollably. He clutched at his stomach as if the laughter was so hard it was beginning to hurt. Just before this, we had been talking about things that Paul liked to do with his dad, such as going for walks, watching TV, joking around and his dad 'teasing' him. I asked him what had made him laugh so suddenly.

In response Paul started imitating my body language and voice, mirroring what I had said very accurately. He pointed at me and started laughing again, in what felt like a cruel, mocking way. I was being teased and wondered if this related to his dad's teasing. I asked if anyone had ever imitated him and he nodded. He stopped laughing abruptly and continued working on his model but after a few moments looked directly at me and said 'heart attack'. I asked if this was what had happened to his dad and Paul said 'yes' in a drawn out, sarcastic tone, looking away from me. The suddenness and violence of his laughter and the clutching of his stomach had made me think of someone experiencing some kind of physical attack over which they had no control, but this contrasted with his controlled and skilful impersonation of me.

Paul again took a book away without asking at the end of the session. It felt as if he was testing the boundaries and my tolerance, perhaps trying to provoke me into anger. In the counter-transference, it connected to feelings of being teased as a child. I wondered if he was including me in his family in some way, perhaps even attempting to recreate the harsh-edged joshing that went on between himself and his father. More ambiguous feelings seemed to be emerging about his relationship with his father, reflected in his impersonations, the objects he made, and his developing relationship with me. As his trust grew in the therapeutic relationship he seemed to be more willing to test it.

In a later session, Paul did a Tommy Cooper impersonation and indicated that his dad used to do this. Tommy Cooper died on stage from a heart attack. I wondered if Paul had heard his dad talking about this and whether it was another link he had made with the sudden loss of his father.

Impersonation

As the therapy continued, more came out about the significance of impersonation for Paul. I realised he had moved on from preoccupation with his father's death and his sense of loss to wanting to talk more about his father in life. One of the things Paul connected with his dad was humour and shared enjoyment of comedians, catchphrases and impersonations. I got a picture in my mind of Paul larking about with his dad, enjoying a laugh. Comedians' catchphrases were perhaps also attractive to Paul as ready-made communication which would elicit recognition and engagement from others. Paul tended to struggle and stutter when he was trying to find fresh words to express himself. He had a series of stock responses, a bit like his own personal catchphrases, which he sometimes used in what seemed like an automatic way such as 'Oh, no!'

Comedians' catchphrases are recognised and enjoyed by many people and are a way of forging bonds with others who are in on the joke and get the reference. In my experience they are particularly enjoyed by men in social situations. Perhaps Paul tried to appeal to his dad through doing impersonations. Paul had also attempted this strategy of engagement through humorous impersonation with people at the day centre but it backfired, with some taking offence and feeling that they were being mocked (many people with learning disabilities are likely to have experienced hurtful imitation by children, and even adults, on the street).

Attachment and identity

Paul's sister had said that his father had found it very difficult to 'accept' Paul as a child with Down's syndrome, he seemed to be ashamed and embarrassed by him. She said her mother took on the majority of care for Paul and she did not remember her father interacting much with him as a child. However, Paul appeared to idolise his dad and thrived on any attention from him, following him around the house when he was at home. After his dad died, Paul lived with his mum and regularly spent time with his sister and nieces, but he had lost the only other man in his immediate family. He seemed to be struggling with his sense of identity as a man without this charismatic role model. His vulnerability since his father's death was most apparent at the day centre, where he had started isolating himself and defending himself with a plastic baseball bat if anyone got too close.

Paul missed several therapy sessions in a row due to transport and escort difficulties. This gap in therapy seemed to bring back some of the feelings of loss and abandonment after his father's death. In the first session after the unplanned break, he walked in and said 'I love you.' I asked if he had been worried he might not see me again and he nodded with his head down. We talked for a while about people he loved including his mum, sister, nieces and father. While we were talking, Paul tenderly shaped an oblong box out of modelling material which he handed to me. He pointed at a drawn image of his dad and made a sad face. I said how hard it must have been not to see his dad again after he suddenly went into hospital. I also commented that he seemed to want to make somewhere comfortable, safe and protected for his father. He nodded. I then linked this to his attempts to find a safe place for himself in the day centre and I said that it must be hard to feel OK without his dad.

Mirror work

Paul became interested in a small mirror in the art therapy room. He pulled faces in the mirror and spent time gazing intently at himself. Paul mimed someone adjusting their glasses and told me that this was his key worker. Then he straightened up and said in a deep voice 'Paul you are a cracker' followed by 'you are a diamond'. He told me that this was his father speaking to him. I wondered if Paul could see his father's features in his own face and asked if he looked like his father but he did not answer. I remembered his sister saying that he was 'similar to his dad in personality'.

According to his key worker, Paul had done some impersonations and mimicking while his father was alive, but these were never impersonations of his father. In the context of the therapy sessions, the impersonations seemed to link closely to his bereavement. Paul's father apparently appreciated his impersonation skills and it was moving to witness Paul recalling his dad's affectionate comments. The therapeutic process seemed to have helped Paul move on from a position of being completely overwhelmed, confused and distraught at the loss of his father to one in which he could share good memories of him.

Paul went on to do impressive impersonations of Bruce Forsyth, Norman Wisdom and Tommy Cooper, all comedians more of his father's generation than his own. I asked Paul if he used to do these impersonations with his father and he nodded, still gazing at his image in the mirror. I said it seemed that he had a lot of good memories of times with his dad, and that he had made his dad laugh. There seemed to be an element of Paul feeling able to keep his dad alive through the impersonations that they used to do together.

I commented that he was good at noticing things about people but that not everyone liked to be imitated. I wondered out loud if some people at the day centre reacted differently to his impersonations and did not get the joke in the way that his father had.

Funeral attendance

Paul then missed an art therapy session due to attending the funeral of a woman from his day centre. Paul had known her but they were not close. His key worker said that Paul attended the whole service and the burial, and had become visibly upset, at times crying behind his hands.

In the following session Paul added a body to an old image of his father's face in the churchyard. He looked at the picture of a coffin in the Mencap leaflet and said it was a 'box'. I asked him about attending the funeral and he said the woman's name and that he had seen her in her 'box'.

Attending the funeral seemed to have a big affect on Paul and his engagement with therapy. He became less interested in using art materials, particularly clay, and stopped making box-like objects. Paul also seemed less preoccupied with his father and spoke more about things which were happening at the day centre.

Review

I attended a review at Paul's day centre before the end of his therapy. Paul, his mum, sister, key worker and psychologist were present. The atmosphere was very tense at the start of the review. With Paul's permission, I fed back in broad terms that Paul was engaging well with art therapy. Paul said that art therapy was 'good' and his mother and sister echoed this, saying he had commented on enjoying the sessions to them too.

Paul's key worker said that there had been a huge improvement in his inter-actions with other people who attended the day centre and that he was now more involved in group activities. The previously escalating 'challenging behaviour' was no longer an issue. Paul had a new programme which included drama sessions which he seemed to love and helped him 'come out of himself'. His support worker also noted an improvement in his concentration and the range of materials he was now using in art classes. There was also discussion about facilitating Paul's wish to visit his father's grave.

Staff were now more understanding about Paul's desire to impersonate people and made an effort to explain to him why people could be upset by this rather than automatically blaming him for bad reactions.

As the key worker spoke there was a tangible thawing of the frosty atmosphere. The family told me later that on all previous occasions when they had been asked to come into the centre, staff had listed Paul's 'bad behaviours' and threatened him with expulsion. In 20 years they could not recall hearing any positive feedback.

The psychologist's work with Paul's wider networks was essential in improving communication between family and staff and in assisting staff in developing a more suitable activity programme. To maximise the positive impact of therapeutic work, it is vital to engage with the people who support the person on a day-to-day basis. If this seems inappropriate, then I suggest working alongside a colleague such as a psychologist (as in this case) who can ensure that issues in the person's wider system of support are addressed.

Feedback from art therapy helped Paul's sister recognise how deeply he had been affected by the loss of his father and by his exclusion from the funeral (which everyone else in the family attended). She later acknowledged that this directly influenced her decision to ensure he attended his mother's funeral a few years later.

There can be a lot of confusion around the issue of confidentiality and privacy in therapy and, of course, the client's consent to share information should always be sought. However, it is important to recognise in working with people with learning disabilities, that significant change for the client is often dependent on influential people in their support network gaining fresh perspectives and insight and sharing their ideas on making change for the better.

Ending therapy

I felt a sense of disengagement come into the therapy sessions, particularly after Paul attended the funeral. He began asking to take artwork away with him at the end of the sessions rather than wanting to leave it with me. Previously, Paul had always put his work in the cupboard or folder; this had felt like an important part of the ceremony of each session: marking the end of a session but also defining a contained, ongoing space for himself and his work within the art therapy room. It was a change that I found quite difficult to accept initially, as I felt that an aspect of my role was to act as a guardian of the objects Paul made representing the loss of his father. Initially, I had the urge to insist on him continuing to leave the artwork. Through discussion in clinical supervision, I realised that it could be viewed as a healthy change, indicating that Paul was feeling more confident and less dependent on me to contain his feelings.

I had been working with Paul for about a year when I heard from the day centre that he had started expressing some reluctance about coming to the sessions. Paul's key worker also said that things were going really well at the day centre; he was joining in with group activities and generally getting on better with people. He had stopped isolating himself and was no longer drawing the repeated image of his father in the churchyard. I began to talk to Paul about the possibility of the sessions ending within the next few months.

The sessions started to feel lighter and more playful. In one session Paul played a mirroring game with me, indicating that he wanted me to copy his exaggerated facial expressions and gestures, laughing with glee the whole time. The cruelty of the previous imitation seemed to have dissipated and this felt more like a reciprocal game about recognising and acknowledging each other.

When working with people who are bereaved, it is obviously important to think carefully about the end of therapy. Paul's father had died quite suddenly and left him in a confused and upset state. I had hoped to work through the ending of therapy with him in a gradual way, acknowledging the difficulties of ending and giving Paul the space to express his feelings about it. Paul knew from the start of therapy that it would not continue forever. Unfortunately, we cannot always have ideal endings in therapy, as in life. In the event, Paul stopped coming to therapy quite abruptly.

I went to the day centre to talk to him about this and Paul and his key worker explained that a new drama session that he was keen to attend was taking place at the time of his therapy. Paul agreed to meet again for one final time to look through the artwork he had made in therapy and review his overall experience of art therapy.

Looking at all the objects he had made (Plate 3.3) seemed to please him. Paul still connected them with his father, pointing at them and saying 'Dad' but he no longer became tearful. He handled the objects gently and put them back into their box and into the cupboard. Paul broke a chocolate bar in two and gave me half before leaving which seemed to be an important, shared gift to mark our parting and the end of the therapeutic relationship.

In my experience, it is quite common for people to precipitate the end of therapy. Paul may have been protecting himself against the pain of the break by engineering it himself, thus gaining some control over the process of ending.

Summary

Art therapy helped Paul mourn and understand the death of his father; literally *shaping his loss* with his hands and clay. It was also crucial that I bore witness to his loss and acknowledged his feelings repeatedly within therapy. In later stages of therapy Paul began to explore more complex, painful feelings about his father, their possibly ambiguous attachment and his identity without 'Dad'.

Paul appeared to have struggled to regain a clear sense of identity as a man since his father's death and had difficulty forming relationships with people outside his immediate family. The skills he had developed in observation and impersonation were a crucial connection to his father but did not seem to have helped Paul when trying to relate to others at the day centre. Reflecting with support staff on the possible functions of impersonation and mimicking for Paul helped them adopt a more understanding perspective on this behaviour rather than just dismissing him as a 'wind-up merchant' as had happened in the past. It also helped staff to think creatively about how Paul might use his impersonation skills, leading to his participation in drama classes.

Within the therapy sessions, my acknowledgement that Paul's impersonations were strongly connected to memories of his father was vital in communicating understanding of his loss. There was a strong link between Paul's physical embodiment of his father through impersonation and the shaping of objects which represented his father in modelling material. The physicality of both media expressed a desire to tangibly hold onto his father and a need for other people to recognise his loss by showing them something real that embodied his feelings. The form of Paul's expression also reflected his learning and communication difficulties. Paul could not express or explain his terrible sense of loss in words but he could communicate it eloquently through art materials and impersonation. Picture books also helped him form a coherent narrative around his traumatic experience.

Working with Paul challenged some of my assumptions about bereavement work. After his mortifyingly accurate imitation of me in the role of sympathetic therapist, I had cause to reflect on how I was positioning myself within the therapeutic relationship. To a large extent I realised I was viewing my role as that of the sympathetic listener, acknowledging Paul's previously ignored sorrow. His humour was an unexpected part of the sessions and ultimately led me to reflect more deeply on his communication and connection with others and more specifically on his relationship with his father.

Paul wanted to entertain and engage others with his impersonations and to demonstrate his skill; he enjoyed laughter and had a wicked sense of humour. It is important to reflect on what lay behind Paul's impersonations but also to recognise the joy and liveliness in them. Paul is a man with strong feelings, he greatly mourned the loss of his father and this was mainly expressed in his manipulation of art materials, which he used to make a safe place for him. Paul demonstrated his loving care for his father in the tender way he shaped objects which represented him and made boxes/coffins to keep him safe.

Later in therapy, Paul was also able to communicate the ongoing pleasure he felt in connecting with his dad through their shared humour. There was a strong sense of Paul keeping his father's presence and memory alive through impersonation of him and his favourite comedians. Although his attachment to his father seems to have contained ambiguities and complications there was clearly real joy in it. Paul taught me not to assume a clear process in bereavement work and that grief can manifest itself in very individual ways.

Postscript

I met Paul and his sister again to ask their permission to write and publish this chapter. Paul had not seen me for several years but he said my name as soon as I arrived and nodded when I asked him if he remembered art therapy. Since the time I worked with him, Paul's mother had died and he was now living with his sister and her family.

Paul's mother had had a longer period of illness than his father and Paul was able to visit her many times in the hospice before she died. Touchingly, his sister said that Paul would often get into bed with his mum for a cuddle at the hospice. He attended his mother's funeral and had visited her grave and his sister said he had shown none of the prolonged confusion, anger and fear that occurred after the death of his father.

Now, Paul regularly goes on holiday abroad with his sister's family and his life has become more active since becoming part of her household. I asked what name

I should use for him in the chapter and he chose Paul, in honour of the musician, Paul Weller.

References

Baum, S. and Lynggaard, H. (2006). *Intellectual Disabilities: A Systemic Approach*. London and New York: Karnac Books.

Blackman, N. (2003). *Loss and Learning Disability*. London: Worth Publishing.

Bowlby, J. (1979). *The Making and Breaking of Affectional Bonds*. London: Tavistock Publications.

Conboy-Hill, S. (1992). 'Grief, Loss and People with Learning Disabilities'. In A. Waitman and S. Conboy-Hill (eds) (1992) *Psychotherapy and Mental Handicap* (pp. 150–170). London: Sage.

Damarell, B. (2007). 'The Supervisor's Eyes'. In J. Schaverian and C. Case (eds) *Supervision of Art Psychotherapy: A Theoretical and Practical Handbook*. London: Routledge.

Emerson, P. (1977). 'Covert Grief Reactions in Mentally Retarded Clients'. *Mental Retardation* 15(6): 46–47.

Grey, R. (2010). *Bereavement, Loss and Learning Disabilities: A Guide For Professionals and Carers*. London and Philadelphia: Jessica Kingsley Publishers.

Hollins, S. and Esterhuyzen, A. (1997). 'Bereavement and Grief in Adults with Learning Disabilities'. *British Journal of Psychiatry* 170: 497–501.

Hollins S. and Sireling, L. (2004). *When Dad Died* (3rd revised edition). London: Gaskell.

Klass, D., Silverman, P. and Nickman, S. (eds) (1996). *Continuing Bonds. New Understandings of Grief*. Phil., PA: Taylor and Francis.

Kuczaj, E. (1998). 'Learning to Say "Goodbye": Loss and Bereavement in Learning Difficulties and the Role of Art Therapy'. In M. Rees (ed.) *Drawing on Difference: Art Therapy with People who have Learning Disabilities*. London: Routledge.

Mattison, V. and Pistrang, N. (2000). *Saying Goodbye When Keyworker Relationships End*. London: Free Association Books.

Oswin, M. (1991). *Am I allowed to cry?* (2nd edition 2000). London: Souvenir Press.

Sinason, S. (1992). *Mental Handicap and The Human Condition: New Approaches From the Tavistock*. London: Free Association Books.

Worden, J. W. (2001). *Grief and Grief Therapy: A Handbook for Mental Health Practitioners* (3rd edition). London: Routledge.

Talking about loss

Janet (Sarah's carer)

. . . but I knew there was underlying issues there and I could see um . . . the problems. One of these problems was that Sarah would go into a shop and she would spend hours if she could just looking at baby food . . . talking to this baby food and reading the contents, reading the ages of it . . . she would look at clothes for babies, she would go through things with me like . . . how long it takes when you're pregnant and how you went through the birth and what was it like and all this . . .

. . . and I was told that she was actually pregnant and had an abortion and then sterilised but there was no record to back this up . . . so it was like a mystery and obviously to me that made sense . . . it was like this lady was grieving you know . . . it was obvious she was grieving for a loss . . .

So the first time art therapy was mentioned?
Well I just thought, what on earth is that . . . it's about art, doing therapy through art and I was like 'great' you know 'she's not going to do this' not really understanding it. I think the first thing was they decided to do an assessment . . .

. . . after realizing that art therapy wasn't about drawing silly pictures, I thought, well OK, if that works it's going to benefit me as well so the home life is going to be different . . . I think I gained from it, she gained from it . . . it was beneficial . . . I think we were just lucky to have that opportunity.

Chapter 4

Leila's shunt

'If I did not have the shunt in my head
I would have been OK'

Stephanie Bull and Emma Shallcross

Introduction

In Chapter 3, Kim Dee discussed Paul's experience of a very specific bereavement but, in this chapter, we want to consider the theme of loss in a more general sense. For anyone with a learning disability, the loss of the 'normal' person is colossal in itself but this can then lead to a deeper sense of loss at each milestone in life not achieved. Kuczaj (1998) writes about a 'loss continuum' where one experience of loss brings about other losses as a consequence. He says that a loss 'has the potential to be a catalyst for other losses, thereby adding to or sometimes confusing further the situation the individual is experiencing' (ibid.: 155).

Here, we look at what happened in Leila's (pseudonym) case when multiple unresolved losses seemed to become fused and enmeshed to form a single *compound loss*. We focus on an image that Leila made while in art therapy with Emma Shallcross which seemed to bring many of her losses together into something that was more tangible and, in this way, perhaps more manageable for her.

Clinical context

The residential home where Leila's art therapy took place was a purpose-built unit for women who had been abused or who were at risk of being abused. The service had been set up in response to the tragic death of a woman with learning disabilities, where the welfare system had failed to support her adequately. The unit provided temporary safe accommodation for women with a range of special needs including mental health problems and learning disabilities. The actual location was not only withheld from abusers but from all people who knew the women including family and friends so loss of relationships was a significant issue for all residents.

The staff worked with each woman to encourage her sense of self-worth and self-respect and to help her develop skills needed to move on to independent living. Each woman was allocated a key worker to support her and assist in accessing a range of relevant services in the areas of employment, health, education and social and leisure opportunities. Art therapy was provided sessionally for any of the women that the staff felt might benefit from it and was in addition to any other support already being provided by the unit.

Initially, Leila was referred to an art therapy assessment group that Emma had set up and the referral was made primarily because staff were finding her behaviour difficult to manage. Leila slammed doors, shouted and threw things in order to let out her rage, anger and frustrations. She seemed unable to channel or express these feelings appropriately and it was thought that art therapy would provide her with expressive opportunities within the safety of the therapeutic boundaries.

Leila's background

Leila was 22 years old and had a mild learning disability. She had been living at the safe house for about 18 months before she began art therapy. She had been born with congenital cerebral palsy which meant that she was unable to fully manage her motor system and, therefore, she was not in control of some movement and muscle tightness. She had a limp which was a direct consequence of her condition. She also had hydrocephalus, which is an accumulation of fluid on the brain and, in her case, this was drained through a shunt (a tube running into her stomach). This shunt later became an important focal point within the therapy. Leila had to be careful with what she ate and had some difficulty swallowing. She also had epilepsy. Unsurprisingly, this multitude of conditions had greatly affected her life, particularly compromising any social opportunities.

It was felt that Leila's family had hindered her development and independence as they claimed that, because she was disabled, she could not do things for herself. They seemed to be convinced that she was weak. Whilst living at the safe house Leila had demonstrated that, in fact, she was strong and also capable of many things, including doing her own shopping and attending college. Leila had eventually been removed from her family's care by social services as there was evidence that some members of the family had been physically abusing her.

Art therapy

The art therapy group ran for 14 weeks and consisted of four women whose ages ranged from 19 to 30 years. Each woman had her own complex issues to work on and these began to be revealed shortly after the group started. The four women already knew each other well as they had lived together in the same environment for some time.

Within the group, Leila often found it difficult to know how to use the art materials and what to draw or paint. Instead, she sometimes chose to help the other women with their image making. Initially, she seemed to present this behaviour as a benevolent and selfless gesture, but it was soon apparent that it was also a strategy for Leila to avoid any focus on her own images and the painful issues that were present for her.

Collectively, similar themes appeared either in conversation or within the image making. However, the women's images seemed to be fairly innocuous whereas their conversations became more and more painful as the group progressed. Whilst the group work helped to bring out each woman's issues to some degree, it did not seem to adequately meet their longer-term therapy needs. When the group came to an end, Leila was offered some individual sessions to give her the opportunity to explore her difficult experiences in greater depth. In the individual sessions, Leila seemed to be far more honest, raw and definitely less polite. Working on a 1:1 basis intensified the therapeutic relationship and the extent of the losses Leila had experienced became much more apparent.

In Leila's case, the loss of her normal self had also meant the loss of place or status within the family. The impact of this seemed to be the loss of healthy relationships with parents and other people in the family. Some family members went on to abuse her which further diminished her self-esteem and sense of self-worth. Eventually she was taken to live at the 'safe house' which then meant the loss of contact with all family members as well as the loss of her familiar objects and environment.

Focusing on disability and physical pain

As the individual sessions progressed, a trusting relationship started to develop and Leila really began to use the sessions. During her ninth individual session, Leila focused on her disabilities, perhaps beginning to explore the original loss she was trying to resolve. She also spoke about how she was feeling physically on that particular day. She said she felt sick and thought that she had a migraine coming. Leila went on to make an image during this session, drawing a picture of the shunt that was implanted in her head with the tube that ran the excess fluid out. This image turned out to be of huge significance (see Figure 4.1 and detail Plate 4.1)

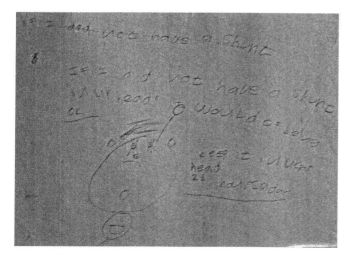

Figure 4.1 Leila: 'If I did not have a shunt in my head I would of been OK'.

Exploring the image's meaning

> A picture is always a great gift to the therapy process: it is an achievement and a creation; it cannot be taken for granted. No matter how elusive it is the picture evokes thoughts and talking about these creates a space for shared viewing and awareness.
>
> (Laine 2007: 125)

We (Stephanie and Emma) have had many discussions over a period of about a year – some face to face and others via email – and have found ourselves returning to Leila's image of the shunt again and again. These discussions took place well after the actual therapy work had finished and were never intended to be supervision sessions as such. However, the opportunity to explore the image together to identify themes and make connections reinforced how clinical supervision can help to deepen our understanding of the person in therapy: 'good supervision is important for working practice and extending the dialogue of understanding' (Case and Dally 1992: 167).

What follows is an edited version of our exploration of the possible meaning and significance of the image of Leila and her shunt.

Stephanie: I am struck by what Leila has written above the figure. 'If I did not have the shunt in my head I would have been OK.' I think it's a really powerful statement.

Emma: She said to me that, if she didn't have a shunt she thought she would be 'normal' and that she envied those who were 'normal'. I remember at the time, feeling that this was somehow aimed at me. If she didn't have the shunt in her head, she thought she would've been loved by her family . . . included by them . . . and that her mother would not have blamed her for existing and for causing the family trouble. The shunt was there to prevent her from getting epileptic seizures so, in reality, the shunt didn't make her disabled . . .

Stephanie: . . . and there's a paradox in the sense that the shunt is what's 'making her OK' but actually, in her experience, it's the shunt that's 'making her not OK'. . . . I wonder if she felt that she wouldn't have suffered the abuse and that, without the shunt, she might have been regarded by her family in an entirely different way?

Emma: I think she thought that, yes . . . this family seemed to want perfection. Her eating problems were due to the shunt and she said she had to be careful not to eat too much but also not to eat too little . . . and because the tube is draining fluid from her brain into her stomach, this often made her feel bloated and sick. Then there was this cycle where she would not want to eat. She just had Coke and chocolates and I felt that this was also another way she would show her anxiety. Her mobility problems were a result of her other condition which was hereditary . . . so any of her siblings could have had it . . .

Stephanie: What would happen to Leila if she had the shunt removed?

Emma: She would probably have a much shorter life. She would get more seizures. . . . perhaps she needs the shunt in another sense . . . to blame . . .

Stephanie: . . . the writing seems really important and I notice that, her first attempt at writing 'If I did not have a shunt' appears to have been crossed out – I wonder why she felt her first attempt wasn't acceptable to her?

Emma: She had realised (without my prompting) that the word 'did' was spelt 'dad' . . . this was her way of correction . . . to cross out the whole thing and start again. Strange, as she wrote it in pencil so it could have been rubbed out rather than corrected . . . it may have been more direct for her to cross out and start again . . . which makes me think of her making a new start in her life at the 'safe house'. In a sense, she has had to cross out everything about her past life – positives and negatives, abusers and loved ones and start again, rearrange her new life at the house . . . correcting it . . .

Stephanie: Does it say 'Keep it inside head 24 hours a day'? or 'Keep it in my head 24 hours a day'?

Emma: . . . she has actually written 'Keep it in my *for* head 24 hours a day' but I think she meant to write, 'Keep it in my head *for* 24 hours a day'. Interestingly, the shunt, while in reality it is further back in her head – where the soft part of her skull is, it does always seem to be in the forefront of her mind in the sense that she's constantly aware of it. It's always there, never leaves her, she is constantly thinking about the shunt and her problems.

Stephanie: It's in there 24/7 . . . she can't take it out . . . and yet looking at her image of herself with the shunt, I'm also struck by how separate it is from her head and body – only connected by a thin line. I wonder why she's not shown it as actually being in her head . . . which is where it is in reality?

Emma: She described the shunt as having a mind of its own . . . only it knew when it was going to hurt. Perhaps this is why the shunt is outside of her. She doesn't understand it; it hurts, does its own thing and causes her pain when it wants to . . .

Stephanie: . . . she's externalised it . . . and that makes me think about what the loss of the 'normal self' really meant to her because, in a sense, the shunt could be seen as the tangible bit of the loss . . . Even though we know it's there to try and save her life . . . it's also something that she feels shouldn't be there . . .

Emma: I commented in my notes at the time that the image looked like an alien and now I'm thinking about it again, it is actually alien to her, it's not a part of her, there's no connection . . . again perhaps a metaphor of her family's view of her. In this session Leila had said she had a headache and I realised how difficult it must have been for

	her to muster up the strength to physically come to the session and share the painful feelings in such distress. The thin line, as you say, does not look like a tube. I would have thought it should be quite substantial as it's like a lifeline connecting her brain and stomach.
Stephanie:	I'm interested in the way she has drawn herself.
Emma:	The person she has drawn is very similar to her other drawings of people which I would describe as quite primitive . . . it's preschematic (there is no baseline or sky so fairly typical of a 3- or 4-year-old child of normal development). It is not in proportion and misses out various details. Perhaps she wants to show a more emotive image emphasising her head, small weak body and even weaker thin and spindly legs . . . looks like there's not enough strength to hold her, she had a limp and required a stick when she walked outside of the house.
Stephanie:	I wonder what it says about her as a woman.
Emma:	The figure is not obviously female. I thought her eyelashes were tears at the time and they seem to be the only thing alluding to her femininity . . . outside of session she smiled a lot actually . . . giving the impression to staff that all was all right . . . I felt she could be more honest with me.

Key themes

Our exploration of Leila's image of her and her shunt enabled us to identify four key themes:

- **The shunt creating a paradox** – the shunt was there to save Leila's life and yet, in doing so, it had a very negative impact on her day-to-day experiences.
- **Multiple losses** – Leila's disabilities and the loss of her normal self seemed to have also brought about loss of status within the family which may have contributed to her becoming the victim of abuse and subsequently losing her home and her possessions.
- **Internal or external?** Was the shunt part of her or was it alien?
- **Self and identity** – Leila's image of herself within therapy. Her sadness, and her vulnerability were in contrast to the image that she presented to others at the safe house.

Unfortunately, it wasn't possible for Emma to develop these themes with Leila at length within the therapy sessions because this work came to an end for funding rather than clinical reasons.

Ending

Emma was invited to a meeting with the Project Manager at the safe house who explained that, for a combination of reasons, there was only funding available for eight more art therapy sessions. Leila's art therapy, whilst having been quite challenging, was really beginning to develop into something important yet Emma had no control over this situation and neither did Leila. Leila had already had a lifetime of having no choice or control.

When Emma told Leila that they would have to bring the therapy to an end, her first reaction was of one panic, fear and despair: 'Who will help me now?' she asked. She said she was worried that her mental health would deteriorate. Leila wrote messages to Emma, sometimes saying 'please do not go' but at other times saying that she could not come to the remaining art therapy sessions as she was finding it difficult to cope with ending the work. However, of the sessions that were remaining, Leila only missed one.

Not long before the final session, Leila spoke about a dream she'd had of being in hospital, adding that she often dreamt of being in hospital when someone she knew was leaving. It was clear by the tone of her voice that she was angry and that she blamed Emma in some way for what she was experiencing. She asked why they had begun art therapy in the first place, believing that Emma had known all along that it would end before she was ready. She threatened to self-harm, run away, throw things in her flat, slam doors and play her music loudly – these being things she used to do before she began having art therapy. There seemed to be an immense feeling of waste.

At one point, Leila said that she wanted to lock Emma in the room to stop her from leaving and she also suggested that they stay in contact via email. Together they explored these intense feelings that she was expressing and Leila eventually told Emma about a tutor at college that she felt had been supportive towards her and had listened. Leila seemed to be letting Emma know, on the one hand, that she (Emma) could be replaced and yet, on the other, Leila may have been trying to reassure Emma that she had support and would be OK.

Outcome

Just over a year later, Emma visited Leila at the safe house to ask her for consent to write about her in this chapter and publish her image. Leila gave her consent, also telling Emma that she would be leaving the safe house the following week as she would be moving into more independent accommodation. She seemed pleased to be moving on at last.

Conclusion

Leila had a significant number of unresolved losses that seemed to have become fused and confused into one complex experience. When there is not enough time between losses to properly grieve and process each one, then thoughts and feelings connect one loss or grief with another and a confusion of overwhelming and intensified emotions can set in.

The impact of *compound loss* is such that the person's sense of self and identity, their relationships with others and their belief frameworks can all become profoundly destabilised. For some, there can also be a lingering sense of being bad and of somehow being the architect of whatever has brought about the losses they have experienced. Leila was literally removed from everything that had been familiar to her and it wasn't surprising that her emotions were overwhelming and somewhat out of control.

Art therapists working with people with learning disabilities frequently encounter those who have experienced complex and multiple losses and it is often difficult to know where and how to focus the therapy – this seemed to happen in the earlier stages of Leila's therapy.

Finding a means of expression was essential for Leila and the opportunity to use image making provided her with a useful way forward. The image of the shunt then became central to her art therapy and seemed to have the capacity to hold and to finally express much of what had become overwhelming and confused in a more manageable and concrete form.

References

Case, C. and Dalley, T. (1992). *The Handbook of Art Therapy*. London: Routledge.
Kuczaj, E. (1998). 'Learning to Say "Goodbye": Loss and Bereavement in Learning Difficulties and the Role of Art Therapy'. In M. Rees (ed.) *Drawing on Difference*. London: Routledge.
Laine, R. (2007). 'Image Consultation: Supporting the Work of Art Therapists'. In J. Schavarien and C. Case (eds) *Supervision of Art Psychotherapy*. London: Routledge.

Talking about ending

Henry

What was the most difficult thing about art therapy?

Ending art therapy – I didn't want to stop.

. . . a bit sad I was . . . we'd been doing it for quite a while . . . talking about

private stuff . . . used the art materials.

I've moved on.

Part III

Attachment and separation

Chapter 5

Skating in the dark

Sandra Storey

Catrin

I can remember you, child,
As I stood in a hot, white
Room at the window watching
The people and cars taking
Turn at the traffic lights.
I can remember you, our first
Fierce confrontation, the tight
Red rope of love which we both
Fought over. It was a square
Environmental blank, disinfected
Of paintings or toys. I wrote
All over the walls with my
Words, coloured the clean squares
With the wild, tender circles
Of our struggle to become
Separate. We want, we shouted,
To be two, to be ourselves.

Neither won nor lost the struggle
In the glass tank clouded with feelings
Which changed us both. Still I am fighting
You off, as you stand there
With your straight, strong, long
Brown hair and your rosy,
Defiant glare, bringing up
From the heart's pool that old rope,
Tightening about my life,
Trailing love and conflict,
As you ask may you skate
In the dark, for one more hour.

                             Gillian Clarke (1985)

Background

In this chapter I would like to consider how images and the therapeutic relationship within which they are created communicate about and address learning disability, attachment and separation. Inherent within attachment and separation is loss (Bowlby 1969, 1973, 1981). It is inextricably linked and therefore evident here. However, it is focused on more specifically in Chapters 3 and 4.

The terms attachment and separation are looked at initially in terms of the traditional understanding of the infant/carer relationship. Later experiences of attachment and separation are then addressed. They have an impact of their own and may reflect or resonate with earlier experiences. An overarching theme within this chapter is how responses to learning disability can lead to an enmeshing of the individual with their carers. I describe how institutionalisation creates additional enmeshment of a different kind.

My intention is to share and illustrate the role that I believe art psychotherapy has to play in giving clients the opportunity to reveal what this means for them and how it is then possible to develop individuality and self-definition. A consideration of separation-individuation as outlined by Mahler *et al.* (1975) is important in coming to an understanding of this.

Introduction

Because of its immediacy I would like to look initially at these issues with the insight of poetry. Gillian Clarke's words at the beginning of this chapter are rich with images, colours and symbols that evoke birth, the struggle for the first separation of mother and daughter and the interlacing of holding on and letting go that follows.

The tightening and loosening of attachments and the tension of dependence and independence is tinged with love and conflict. I have worked with a number of women where these conflicts are at the heart of what is revealed in the artwork and in the therapeutic relationship. The significant and additional theme explored in this chapter compared to that of the poem is that the women have a learning disability. Gillian Clarke's daughter defiantly asks to skate in the dark for one more hour tightening her mother's wish to protect, to be attached, and to prevent harm. I hope to explore here how having a learning disability can sometimes affect the way that attachments evolve and how the negotiation of separation is coloured with the response to dealing with learning disability (Storey 1996).

In work which took place with people moving on from an institutional setting the therapeutic relationship often became a vessel in which the 'struggle to become separate' could take place. The images provided a secure base where these embryonic changes were initially expressed. Further growth was reflected in verbalisation and resonances between the image and therapeutic relationship. The metaphorical or indeed real request to 'skate in the dark for one more hour' is likely to provoke additional feelings if concerns for the individual's vulnerability and capacity to manage independently are already heightened. Perhaps more poignantly, it is the growth of curiosity and emergence of the desire to explore what skating in the dark might be like which is sometimes hindered.[1] The question embodies a request for freedom, separation, risk taking and steps into an exciting and potentially hazardous new world. It is often not asked and does not have the opportunity to form itself.

Making images within a secure and supportive relationship offers the duality of containment and recognition of the individual. New thinking, curiosity and imagery can then evolve: questions can be asked. I will look at the evidence I have seen for this through three case studies and descriptions of relevant theory.

The groups which have particularly highlighted these processes are as follows:

- **Mothers and daughters** – A number of women referred for art psychotherapy assessment with varied emotional difficulties have reflected on some common themes. This is seen in underpinning issues related to individuation, independence, individuality and their relationships with their mothers.
- **Institutions and individuals** – A number of people with a learning disability who had originally lived in a large hospital went on to move into their own homes, with support, in the community. Some of these people were seen for art psychotherapy assessment and ongoing work. The focus was on the merging of individual and institution and the struggle to separate. Attachment issues and the way in which separation and individuation were impacted on are at the heart of this therapeutic work.

Theoretical influences

Art psychotherapy and learning disability

The relevance of art psychotherapy for people with a learning disability was highlighted by Rees *et al*. in 1998. It is regarded as a safe and supportive setting where people can creatively discover their capacity to 'think' (Stack 1996), make sense of their experiences (Tipple 1994), and where attachment issues can be safely addressed.

With regard to learning disability, it was not until the 1970s that momentum began to gather on the recognition of emotional needs. There was a growing awareness that emotional experiences remain intact regardless of intellectual disability (Oswin 1973; Symington 1981; Bicknell 1983). There was a growing awareness also that societal attitudes and responses to disability can create a 'secondary disability' (Sinason 1992) as can the impact of institutional life because of the separations and losses it forces (Bowlby 1969, 1973, 1981). Chapter 2 provides further theoretical insights into the experience of having a learning disability.

The significance of attachment theory

Fundamental to this chapter are insights from attachment theory. Briefly put, attachment theory considers how behaviour evolves between parents/caregivers and children which has the function of both protecting the child but affording it enough of a secure base to explore new situations safely. Further, it considers how the capacity for exploration and curiosity are hampered when the emotional base of the child is not secure. I will look later at current perspectives on parental response and adaptation to a diagnosis of learning disability and the links to insecure attachment. This is an important link when considering how new learning and the forming of a sense of self evolve. Additionally, this can overshadow, or is confused with, the existing learning disability.

The significance of separation and separation-individuation

In the following case studies separation is important in the sense that Bowlby and other attachment theorists have described. By this I mean the impact of separation on attachment relationships.

Separation-individuation theory is also highly relevant and meaningful here. Mahler *et al.* (1975) describe the development of a sense of self which includes initial symbiotic phases in infant development where the young infant perceives itself to be as one with the mother. Over an evolving period the child begins to distinguish itself from mother/carer and to achieve a sense of individuality. A 'psychological birth' is described which is the conceptual equivalent of the cutting of the umbilical cord. Individuation requires a process of gradual emotional separation which continues in later years (for example, adolescence). If individuation requires decreased dependence on caregivers and increased independence then there are clear considerations here for clients with leaning disabilities who, for a variety of reasons, experience obstacles to this process.

It has been proposed that 'whereas Bowlby delineated the impact of actual separation from the mother, Mahler conceptualised separateness in the presence of the mother' (Blum 2004: 544).

Whilst Bowlby and other attachment theorists have focused largely on observable, scientific evidence, Mahler has brought a greater focus to the unconscious lives of infant and carer. There is a great deal of debate around these ideas which can only be referenced here. Although there appear to be many differences and commonalities between attachment theory and psychoanalysis all are joined in the belief that:

> the psychological self develops through perception of oneself in another person's mind as thinking and feeling. Parents who cannot reflect with understanding on their child's inner experience and respond accordingly deprive the child of a core psychological structure that he or she needs to build a viable sense of self.
>
> (Fonagy 2001: 167)

Therapeutic work

Judy

I worked with Judy over a two-year period. She was referred to art psychotherapy initially with regard to the impact of previous traumatic experiences.

Judy was forty-five years old and had lived with her family until late adult life. She had often shared a bed with her mother as an adult. She talked about words that her mother had used when describing her appearance when she was born which implied difference and strangeness. She believed that this was true. Judy never discussed this with me with any malicious emphasis or sense of indignation but simply as a passing on of fact. A major part of our work together was on her developing sense of separateness. It was as if mother and daughter existed in a symbiotic relationship. The images Judy made were clear and important statements of self. They were filled with exotic creatures who had to kill each other to survive. They would either eat or be eaten. Judy's mother's health had been deteriorating and separation had been anticipated for some time. They were likely to be living in separate accommodation in the future. There were many mixed and complex emotions leading up to this. However, some time after the separation took place Judy began to introduce humans to her images for the first time. They were walking into the sea (Plate 5.1) and she spoke clearly about her relationship with her mother. On one occasion she told me 'when I look in the mirror I see her' (meaning her mother). There is an absence of her self and a sense that her evolving self was not mirrored in a way that nurtured her separate identity. The work that followed suggested a need to merge with or possibly re-internalise her mother. In the artwork this was seen in Judy's resistance to making new images and in a wish to rework old images as if trying to merge with or forge new ways of internalising the past. Within the therapeutic relationship and other relationships modifications continue to happen and new internalisations take place (Reed 2006). The image offers a safe place for initial expression and exploration of this.

Winnicott suggests that 'the precursor of the mirror is the mother's own face' (Winnicott 1971: 130) and Mahler describes the importance of separation from mother in the move towards individuation. What is described initially by Judy is a feeling of still being merged. Her own image/sense of identity has been overwhelmed by that of her mother. However, the move from animal to human imagery and Judy's increased ability to verbalise feelings about closeness and separation with her mother indicate a new feeling of understanding and self-definition.

Early emotional responses to learning disability

For a person born with an evident disability the impact of loss may begin at birth. Joan Bicknell describes the experience of families whose children have had disabilities. She describes this very powerfully by using the words of a mother who had this experience. Her words express the sense of bereavement and grief, the loss of the baby who had been dreamed about and expected and the adapting to the different baby who arrived. 'Whenever I hear James cry, I hear *his* cry, but I also hear the perfect cry, of the perfect baby I never had' (Bicknell 1983: 167).

Although loved, protected and regarded as special as any new baby might be, there is a process of adapting which has to take place here, which to varying degrees will include the experience of loss. Bicknell goes on to describe other experiences of loss, for example when recognition of disability evolves slowly. It is impossible to think about these first experiences of loss without thinking about what the baby internalises about itself, what it sees first in the maternal gaze and then in the gaze of others. What is especially significant here is that the attachment process may be damaged, as is the process of disillusionment which is important in the process of separation (Winnicott, 1971).[2] Stokes and Sinason (1992) outline ways in which separation can become complicated. There may be an unconscious fear for the child (and developing adult) that separation will bring rejection. This is somehow avoided if the child can continue with the fantasy that she/he is still merged with the caregiver. They also suggest that separation can mean facing the depression linked with feelings of loss engendered by the impact of disability. Non-separation can be a way to avoid facing the potentially painful impact of disability. Where attachments are not secure and when there are difficulties in moving from illusion to disillusion the potential for exploration and curiosity may be hindered and separation compromised.

Within the framework of attachment theory Oppenheim *et al.* (2007: 131) focus on the impact of parental resolution on the developing child with a learning disability. Parental resolution refers to the process, for parents, of coping with their emotional responses to the diagnosis of learning disability and adapting to the needs of their child. Parents who are unresolved about their child's diagnosis are less able to revise their understanding and adapt to the new reality. This makes the parent less able to 'read the child's signals correctly and respond in appropriate ways'.

Marvin and Pianta (1996) describe the relationship between feelings of loss and grief regarding a diagnosis of cerebral palsy and the impact on parent/child relationships. Results and conclusions included that parents who had adapted to and were resolved about the diagnosis were strongly associated with secure child–parent attachment whereas parents who were unable to adapt and cope with their emotional responses were strongly associated with insecure child–parent attachment.

Bowlby's work on the grief which follows loss closely informs all the above work.

Ruth

Ruth's father had died and she lived a quiet life with her mother. She was referred for art psychotherapy assessment as she had become increasingly anxious and withdrawn. Ruth found it difficult to express feelings. She was often heard muttering to herself but was rarely able to share concerns with others. Despite being an able person with a mild learning disability she had not had the opportunity to live independently of her family. Sandra Goody focuses on the theme of infantilisation in Chapter 6 and this was certainly an issue for Judy whose skills, abilities and potential for independence appeared not to have been fully recognised. There can be an unconscious collusion between parent and child which denies adulthood because of the anxieties regarding independence and all it entails. This can include sexuality, independence and knowledge of loss (Stokes and Sinason 1992). Skating in the dark is not conceivable.

Ruth was nearly 50 years old when we met for the first time. In the early assessment sessions she conveyed her regimented life through images made with templates. These templates were provided by a support worker who had given them to Ruth just prior to her attending her first session. Although the templates had at first seemed to me to be an intrusion on Ruth's own potential to communicate, they became a very valuable instrument for us through which to understand her dilemma. The first template was of a house and Ruth filled this in over a number of sessions. In so doing she unwittingly, unconsciously, expressed her discomfort with the tension between accepting life as an exercise in fitting a template created by others or alternatively carving out her own individual shape or template. This was made explicit when we worked on a squiggle game together as a way to resolve her fear of moving on from the templates. In this game I made a mark and she turned the mark or squiggle into something new and vice versa. Ruth could not turn my marks into anything and chose instead to replicate them.

Ruth did become more curious about the room we were using and, in time, created her own templates made from scraps of paper. They became representative of her leg, her arm and hand. She used the shape of the scraps to dictate an outline for her in which the body part shape went. Eventually she used the bits of paper she had drawn inside as a further template which she then drew around to give her another outline. Finally, she created a robot out of scraps of paper. She entitled it 'A robot, rather angry', and this third person representation of a creature angered by the fact that it had to respond without will or design to the wishes of others finally allowed her to recognise and give voice to her own frustration. However, this was at some cost.

At the heart of her dilemma was a relationship with her mother which in many ways felt like the umbilical cord between them had not been cut. She felt disloyal and worried about expressing negative emotions about her mother and could not find the words to express her feelings until she made an image of a boat at sea and in some danger. This allowed us to talk about her sense of danger. We could then think together about the possibility of feeling separate emotionally without either mother or daughter experiencing it as a rejection. This was frightening territory for Ruth and we had to seriously consider whether therapy could progress. After this she made a sequence of images which depicted animals in pairs. These were usually a mother and a baby; the baby was an exact replica of the mother (Plate 5.2). It is ironic that Ruth was now liberated to make her images; she no longer needed physical templates. However, the liberation enabled her to make images of her own internalised template: the image of mother and daughter as indistinguishable.

Orbach and Eichenbaum (1987) look from a feminist perspective at the issues faced by any mother and daughter within the process of emotional separation. They describe the cultural, social and parental forces at work on the developing psyche of the daughter. Mother is more likely to identify with daughter as they are of the same gender and the mother may project aspects of herself onto her daughter. Orbach and Eichenbaum suggest that the unnurtured mother, tired from caregiving, teaches her daughter to be caring to others and in so doing becomes a candidate for her daughter's care. 'A cycle in which "giving" occurs out of unmet personal needs is thus set in train. The mother becomes the daughter's first child' (ibid.: 60).

Ruth moved from the pairs to an image about the loss of her father. It was a precious memory of the activities they enjoyed together before Christmas, the festive rituals they enjoyed and time spent together. Although able to tell me about the sadness at church after his funeral, she quickly told me she was happy now.

Our work continued for approximately eighteen months and Ruth's images began to vary. She introduced Valentine cards, fruit, butterflies and plants. We began to talk about her sense of herself as a woman and before our work ended we were also able to look at how the transference aspects of our work (initially expressed through her criticisms of me) had held and supported emotional change. Denial featured oppressively and powerfully in Ruth's life. It required a symbolic process with a non-verbal emphasis to enable this to emerge in a way that she could tolerate emotionally. The umbilical cord was in many ways still intact and metaphorically speaking could not have been cut without first having 'the struggle to become separate . . . To be two, to be ourselves' (Clarke 1985).

'Our house is our corner of the world . . . it is our first universe' (Bachelard 1964)

I would like to draw attention to adult experiences of attachment and separation and how a sense of self and individuality can be lost or enmeshed in an institutional setting. This is often in addition to early and/or repeated experiences of separation and loss. An overshadowing of the original disability can take place which further impacts on the development of self and identity.

This is, of course, essentially different from the difficulties encountered in nego-tiating separation between mother and daughter as previously discussed. However, my experience of working with both these groups of people was that the art psychotherapy process provided a setting where complex, subtle and embryonic material related to attachment and separation could be expressed. This then paved a way towards increased individuation and self-definition. Clients could form questions and take risks both real and metaphorical – some of which may well have felt like 'skating in the dark'. The defiance of the skater may previously have had more opportunity for expression through challenging behaviour than in a negotiated relationship where transformation could evolve.

It is interesting to reflect on the fact that art therapy had its beginnings within large institutional settings (Hill 1951). Its aims always included the development of choice, independence, self-expression/-exploration and control. In particular, creative means have been used to facilitate the expression of individuality in institutional environments where this has often been repressed (Stott and Males 1984).

Referral

A referral was made to art psychotherapy for assessment to be offered to people with a learning disability who had originally lived in a large hospital and then in special needs units which were health service based. At the time of referral they were about to move into their own homes, with support, in the community. The intention was to address the emotional impact of the losses and adjustments experienced in this process. The process of moving from one home to another happened to a group of people, as described previously, so it makes sense to look first at some of the common issues and then, specifically, at the experience of one person.

Assessment

The assessment process began five to six months before the move to the new houses took place. Some, but not all, of those referred to art psychotherapy continued with ongoing therapeutic work. This varied from six to seventeen months in length and was determined through regular review of the work with clients and key members of staff.

The sessions took place on a weekly, individual basis at the same time and in the same place each week. This is a basic principle of practice but was especially important to these men who were adapting from a known and familiar experience to an unknown situation with some unknown people. They were also experiencing the loss of people to whom they had become attached.

The clients had already experienced separation as an intrinsic part of going to live in an institutional setting. The attachments that were then formed to the institution and to the people who worked and lived there with them were charged with this experience of separation.

Each person who engaged in art psychotherapy found unique ways of making it a supportive experience. They were able to forge new ways of expressing complex emotions and developed an increased capacity to reflect on and make sense of them. Although this happened in different ways for each person there were some common features which included value of a neutral space for 'thinking', promotion of language and insight and an increase in expression of perceived negative emotion, for example anger and sadness.[3] These were identified within therapy but also through feedback from staff who were involved and additionally through semi-structured interviews which were transcribed and analysed. This took place as part of a service evaluation which looked at the experience of the move for all concerned (Storey and Davey 2008).

Therapeutic work

George

George is a man who was originally admitted to a long-stay hospital in his early twenties. George found expression of emotion difficult. He had made strong attachments to some members of staff and to other particular residents. He had been known to be challenging and aggressive. As a child he did not achieve single-word communication until age four and it is noted that he made no progress in mainstream schools.

When we first met, George was uncomfortable about remaining alone in a room with me and the assessment period often involved an invitation to one of the staff members to join us for part of the session. This became an essential part of the work. The boundaries of the session meant that we had a metaphor for the move that George was about to go through. That is to say we had made a frame, a new setting for him, in the shape of the sessions into which he could place his anxieties, unconscious and conscious, about how it felt to make the move to a new setting, his home to be.

We agreed that the assessment would take place at the health based setting where George currently lived but was due to move from. This setting would be closing and we would negotiate a new setting after the assessment.

George conveyed his anxiety about moving home strongly, often requesting that staff join us in the session. When it was intolerable for him to bear the feelings about this with me alone we included a staff member not just for reassurance and support but also so that George could ask some of the questions that he was beginning to form during therapy and to which he needed practical answers. This phase took place prior to the move itself.

Introducing art materials was interesting for George. He liked to have them there and to have them pointed out but he was reluctant to attempt anything by himself and resisted them over a number of sessions. He preferred the idea of instructing me to use them with ideas that he had had. After initial qualms it seemed to me that this was the way ahead for symbolic expression. He had ideas inspired by the presence of art materials and by the regular presence of someone who was willing to find creative and adaptive ways for him to communicate feelings that so far had no shape. The fact that I may have had to make them based on his instruction also communicated about institutional ways of relating. It was a change of role and allowed something new to emerge. It wasn't until later in therapy that we were able to explore ways of relating. What emerged initially were institutional cultures of demanding and being demanded of as opposed to negotiation. It is of course important that we considered all factors that may impede communication. George communicated effectively with limited vocabulary. However, as therapy progressed the way in which he related to me changed as did his wish and ability to communicate. His vocabulary increased both verbally and pictorially.

Initially I felt that I was related to as an extension of him in the way that Hollins *et al.* (1994) describe the need for an 'auxiliary' brain until the person is ready to take over and manage this function themselves. Mahler's reflections on merged states may also be relevant here. Previous experiences and impact of institutional-isation also affect the capacity for independent thinking and action.

Schneider (1992) looks at the way in which separation-individuation theory helped in the planning of transition and changes in the lives of emotionally dis-turbed young adults. Some emphasis is placed on consideration of whether the young people are in a merged or 'symbiotic' phase in which case they may look to the clinician too eagerly, 'feeling secure in having someone tell them what to do'. However, it is suggested that lack of instruction will make decisions hard for the young person who is not emotionally prepared for them.

In one of the early sessions I made a template of a man which was a jointly negotiated process. George was able to talk about the different functions and senses that this man, symbolic of him, would need to manage the transition he was about to go through. He identified features for the person and considered the emotions he might experience: worry in his stomach and a brain to help him think. His mouth is closed as he does not like shouting. We often referred back to this image in particular as the worried stomach was a shorthand symbol for him or me to refer to worried feelings.

As sessions progressed George no longer needed to have a staff member present and he became more curious about the art materials and how to use them himself. The initial ideas were sometimes themes or directions from me because at this early stage he found engagement without this support impossible and again I thought about the impact of institutionalisation and the way in which a sense of self had been lost or merged with the institution.

The frame and container of the sessions themselves allowed other frames and containers to develop. For example, we developed a box together. It had a lid which George decorated and in which he kept any scraps, templates or small pieces of work from the sessions. This also reverberated as a symbol for his transition. He could hold onto important objects and move them from one place to another.

We moved from the original base for therapy about three months after starting. It was important to think carefully about doing this because of the resonances with loss and change that we were already working with. A date was set which would be some time prior to George's actual move.

The new venue coincided with an increase in curiosity and independent work in the sessions. Also, George introduced new characters to his images. Largely they were the characters who peopled his life. He would have to say goodbye to some but would continue contact with others. George had made particular attachments both to residents and to staff.

Joint work where we played squiggle games together promoted George's sense of playfulness with imagery and also developed his capacity to verbalise his thoughts. For example, I had begun to reflect on George's relative quietness in the sessions and the fact that I talked more and asked more questions. George responded to this by saying:

'You've got more to talk about than me.'

After initial consideration of this I reflected on George's age and mine; on the fact that he had lived for about thirty years more and the potential this gave for many things to talk about. It is painful in retrospect to consider that although I connected with feelings about institutionalisation and therefore a sense of not having anything to talk about, my response fell far short of recognising the sheer weight of lost experiences and low self-esteem which I believe George was also referring to. It was only when away from George, reflecting on this by writing up notes and in clinical supervision, that I could contemplate the magnitude of it. My own age was also the amount of time that George had spent in institutional care. It is significant that around this period in therapy George began to vocalise the importance of his intimate attachment to a close friend and to other relationships as described above.

It was also the start of more verbalised transference work and a recognition of George's increased 'mindfulness'. As George became more vocal and I became more attuned it was easier to see patterns of relating developing. For example, George would order me to pass, do or get things for him. 'You do it', was a common demand. Conversely, he would at times put me in a position of authority, investing in me the authority he had assumed from others in an institutional setting. In response to my invitations he would often say:

'Don't know what to do' or 'Anything.'

It was a gradual recognition of this that enabled him to verbalise and share the feeling of:

'You've got more to talk about than me.'

Here George is able to think about himself and me, to contemplate the differences and similarities. He is able to communicate this and to convey his sense of loss and experience of hierarchy.

Transference aspects of the work and adaptations to art psychotherapy practice

The impact of institutionalisation on relating and on relationships became increasingly evident through the therapeutic relationship. George viewed me as an authority figure and sometimes as an extension or merged part of himself which he wanted to control. This was not linear, it ebbed and flowed, but George was more able to reflect on and modify these processes as time went on.

I initially directed and led the work using templates and offering themes to work with. This was a conscious and considered response though in itself a counter-transference response of sorts. Although necessary, it was influenced by past patterns of relating and was influential on new patterns of relating. I failed to fully recognise the communication of loss being made on the occasion recorded above. This gave way in later sessions to an experience of attunement. In this phase I experienced being demanded of and was aware of attempts to control me. Our reflections on these processes in very simple words meant that George could consider his anticipation of control from me and we could both adapt our ways of relating. Images made when transference issues were becoming more conscious are largely conceived and executed by George himself. He made choices about which materials to use and was able to initiate emotionally difficult subjects, for example he talked to me about going to a recent funeral and introduced an image of his own hand, his individual stamp, which he had drawn around. The content of the sessions generally reveal a continued increase in playfulness, experimentation and confidence with the materials. He begins to add himself and his name to the imagery.

On many occasions I felt that I was stretching the usual boundaries of art psychotherapy to breaking point. How far could the frame of therapeutic work be pushed out of shape before it became insecure? However, to be able to offer a therapeutic experience to George required adaptations to practice. To include other staff members in the way I have described, to produce images at his instruction and to be so directive in the early sessions were essential in terms of an attuned response which allowed him to progress to greater autonomy at a later stage. These adaptations required careful reflection, attention to my own responses and skilful supervision.

Ending and separating

Negotiating the ending was, of course, crucially important. Regular reviews always offered the opportunity to consider this. As George became more open and verbal we were more able to 'be separate, to be ourselves' (Clarke 1985) and this made consideration of ending a possibility. In one review I drew a long pencil line with the beginning and end indicated. I asked George to show me, on the line, how far he thought we had gone in therapy and how far we had left to go. He made a mark somewhere near the end, very much what I would also have estimated. He then threw my understanding by adding a mark close to the beginning too. Although the complexity of this needed to be weighed up it set in motion a contemplation of separation. We ultimately negotiated a carefully considered ending. This included a concrete representation of how many sessions were left. In the final images George made drawings of me and I had to guess their identity. We have received separate definition; George's hand and my face are placed in the same image. There is no sense of merging here. In another image he tells me he has given me a toilet. He was not able to explore this verbally with me but the resonances are irresistible. It felt strangely intimate, potentially infantilising, and a little intrusive possibly. It was certainly revealing of his capacity to think about my basic needs. A toilet is also a place for waste after the sustaining elements of food have been digested and processed.

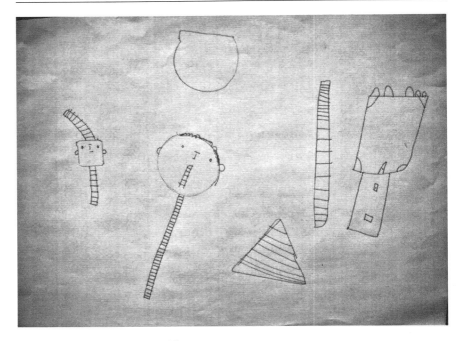

Figure 5.1 George: Ladders and faces.

George's symbols, witnessed in his images and in his language, communicate his capacity to emerge from the institution and to find self-definition. He is aware of his mind and mine and makes efforts to communicate this to me.

George also introduced ladders and people wearing hats. The link between hats and authority is hard to miss. However, as I reflect on this last period of work I also note the quietness and, on some occasions, a flavour that we had returned to the beginning. I was aware that I felt, but resisted, the need to become more directive again. This is echoed in George's indication on the line I drew for him of where he feels he is in therapy time-wise. He is near the end but also near the beginning.

Conclusion

Symbolic work and change

Art therapists aim to establish supportive, therapeutic relationships which facilitate the creation of symbols and metaphors. This expression gives birth to new understanding and change. In addition to this Margaret Wilkinson's contribution to contemporary neuroscience highlights the way in which 'symbolic metaphors not only announce change but enable it' (Wilkinson 2007: 325). This is now evidenced through increasingly sophisticated developments in ways to look at brain activity and the mind-brain understanding which has followed. What is of particular interest here is that 'changes will occur in the configurations of both mind and brain in client and in therapist as new neural connections are made as a result of their interactions' (Wilkinson 2006: 3). She states, 'In therapy, a new experience of relating enables the development of a secure attachment style and, consequently, a more coherent sense of self' (Wilkinson 2007: 329). These ideas are highly relevant to learning disability where attachment is often a complex area. Intellectual capacity can be impacted on through secondary disability and trauma. It is evident then that this is available to change through therapeutic engagement and symbolic work.

Mentalisation has further insights to offer. Mentalisation is 'a specific symbolic function that is central to both psychoanalysis and attachment theory' (Fonagy 2001). It is often defined as seeing ourselves from the outside and others from the inside. Fonagy suggests that psychotherapy enhances mentalisation by activating the attachment system. Work done by art psychotherapists evidences how the image can become central in this process 'enabling clients to observe their sense of self emerging along with others perceiving them as thinking and feeling' (Franks and Whitaker 2007).

In summary, I have aimed to cast light on aspects of my clinical work that are often elusive. To do this, I have brought together wide and varied ways to think about how relationships past and present have impacted on some of the clients I have met. In particular, on how having a learning disability affects relationships, attachment and separation, throughout the lifespan. The clients whose experiences I have highlighted here communicate a sense of being enmeshed or merged and are seen to gradually move closer to self-definition.

When we sit down together for the first time to consider what has brought the person to art psychotherapy a new relationship is offered. It is not only supportive and modifying in itself but it also holds, processes and reflects the impact and expectations created through previous relationships, as does the image.

With these people I have seen images become mirrors and containers which pave the way for the therapeutic relationship to provide mirroring and containment too. The recognition of self and other ebbs and flows but sets in motion an experience of relatedness which enables self-definition and individuality to evolve.

Notes

1 Wordsworth uses the metaphor of skating in the dark in his semi-autobiographical poem, *The Prelude*. He describes the excitement and pleasure of cutting away from the lights of home and even straying from the friends he is with for more solitary exploration.
2 Illusion describes the child's initial experience of feeling not separate from the caregiver and disillusion describes the gradual realisation that they are separate.
3 The attack on 'thinking' through institutionalisation, societal attitudes and psychological responses to learning disability is acknowledged and explored by numerous clinicians and writers: McCormack 1991; Sinason 1992; Stack 1996.

References

Bachelard, G. (1964). *The Poetics of Space*. New York: The Orion Press Inc. (Translation).

Bicknell, J. (1983). 'The Psychopathology of Handicap', *British Journal of Medical Psychology* 56: 167–178.

Blackman, N. (2003). *Loss and Learning Disability*. London: Worth Publishing.

Blum, H. (2004). 'Separation – Individuation Theory and Attachment Theory', *Journal of the American Psychoanalytic Association* 52, 2: 535–553.

Bowlby, J. (1969). *Attachment and Loss, vol. 1, Attachment*. London: Penguin Books.

Bowlby, J. (1973). *Attachment and Loss, vol. 2, Separation*. London: Penguin Books.

Bowlby, J. (1981). *Attachment and Loss, vol. 3, Loss*. London: Penguin Books.

Clarke, G. (1985). *Selected Poems*. Manchester: Carcanet. (First published in 1978 in *The Sundial*. Wales: Gomer Press.)

Fonagy, P. (2001). *Attachment Theory and Psychoanalysis*. New York: Other Press.

Franks, M. and Whitaker, R. (2007). 'The Image, Mentalisation and Group Art Psychotherapy', *International Journal of Art Therapy* 12, 1: 3–16.

Hollins, S., Sinason, V. and Thompson, S. (1994). 'Individual, Group and Family Psychotherapy', in N. Bouras (ed.) *Mental Health in Mental Retardation: Recent Advances and Practices*, pp. 233–243. Cambridge: Cambridge University Press.

Hill, A. (1951). *Painting out Illness*. London: Williams and Norgate.

Mahler, M. S., Pine, F. and Bergman, A. (1975). *The Psychological Birth of the Infant: Symbiosis and Individuation*. London: Hutchinson.

Marvin, R. S. and Pianta, R. C. (1996). 'Mothers' Reactions to their Child's Diagnosis:
Relations with Security of Attachment', *Journal of Clinical Child Psychology* 25, 4: 436–445.

McCormack, B. (1991). 'Thinking, Discourse and the Denial of History: Psychodynamic Aspects of Mental Handicap', *Irish Journal of Psychological Medicine* 8: 59–64.

Oppenheim, D., Dolev, S., Koren-Karie, N., Sher-Censor, E., Yirmiya, N. and Saloman, S. (2007). 'Parental Resolution of the Child's Diagnosis and the Parent-Child Relationship', in D. Oppenheim and D. Goldsmith (eds) *Attachment Theory in Clinical Work with Children*, p. 131. New York: The Guilford Press.

Orbach, S. and Eichenbaum, L. (1987). 'Separation and Intimacy: Crucial Practice Issues in Working with Women in Therapy', in S. Ernst and M. Maguire (eds) *Living with the Sphinx. Papers from the Women's Therapy Centre*. London: Women's Press Ltd.

Oswin, M. (1973). *The Empty Hours. Weekend Life of Handicapped Children in Institutions*. London: Pelican.

Reed, K. (2006). 'Mothers and Daughters', *Journal of the American Psychoanalytic Association* 54, 4: 1245–1256.

Rees, M. (ed.) (1998) *Drawing On Difference: Art Therapy with People who have Learning Difficulties*. London: Routledge.

Schneider, S. (1992). 'Separation and Individuation Issues in Psychosocial Rehabilitation', *Adolescence* Spring 27: 105.

Sinason, V. (1992). *Mental Handicap and the Human Condition. New Approaches from the Tavistock*. London: Free Association Books.

Stack, M. (1996). 'Humpty Dumpty Has a Great Fall', *The Journal of the British Association of Art Therapists* 1, 1: 1–13.

Stokes, J. and Sinason, V. (1992). 'Secondary Mental Handicap as a Defence', in A. Waitman and S. Conboy-Hill (eds) *Psychotherapy and Mental Handicap*. London: Sage.

Storey, S. and Davey, C. (2008). 'A Review on the Transition from a Health Model of Care to Supported Living for Adults with Learning Disabilities in Craven and Harrogate'. Local service evaluation for the Craven and Harrogate Partnership Board. Unpublished.

Storey, S. (1996). 'Art Therapy with People who have Learning Disabilities'. Presented at: Against the Odds – Art Education and Special Needs, Bretton Hall, West Yorkshire. Unpublished.

Stott, J. and Males, B. (1984). 'Art Therapy for People who are Mentally Handicapped', in T. Daley (ed.) *Art as Therapy*. London: Tavistock Publications.

Symington, N. (1981). 'The Psychotherapy of a Subnormal Patient', *British Journal of Medical Psychology* 54: 187–199.

Tipple, R. (1994). 'Communication and Interpretation in ArtTherapy with People who have a Learning Disability', *The Journal of the British Association of Art Therapists* 2: 31–35.

Wilkinson, M. (2006). *Coming into Mind. The Mind-Brain Relationship: A Jungian Clinical Perspective*. London: Routledge.

Wilkinson, M. (2007). 'Coming into Mind Contemporary Neuroscience, Attachment, and the Psychological Therapies: A Clinical Perspective', *New Directions in Psychotherapy and Relational Psychoanalysis* 1: 323–330.

Winnicott, D. W. (1971). *Playing and Reality*. London: Tavistock.

Part IV

Infantilisation

Chapter 6

Stuck in childhood?

Sandra Goody

Introduction

Infantilisation is a word that describes the holding back of maturity. Being 'infantilised' or 'infantilising' oneself can result in dependencies which are unnecessary, a state of being unskilled where independence is resisted and separation is avoided. For a person with a learning disability the tasks which aid independence may be harder to acquire or may not be able to be acquired. Those who support the person with a learning disability may have a diminished sense of hope for their future and this in turn may lead them to keep the disabled person in a protected childlike state. The disabled person can collude with these stagnant levels of dependency as a means of avoiding the pain and fear surrounding the risks needed when new skills are called upon.

The development theory of Kohut and self-psychology (Kohut 1971: 74–86) is helpful as there is less emphasis on childhood as the dominant period of development, suggesting that the need for relationships with self-objects continues throughout the lifespan. This seems a comforting theory when working with people whose development is cognitively delayed and who will inevitably make slower progress. Winnicott's developmental theories (Abram 1996: 130) see the 'journey through dependence' towards independence and the achievement that we accept our self as different from others as key. Through empathic parenting and relationships we negotiate our way through, initially, our desire to be omnipotently 'mirrored' by idealised 'self-objects' into tolerating frustration through developing the capacity for self-soothing, which we learn from empathic nurturing. Kohut describes 'tolerable disappointments' (Kohut 1971: 63–67) as being necessary to development as it is through these that the capacity for self-soothing is learned. One's toleration of being separate is developed through the capacity to self-soothe.

Remaining as a child or regressing into a childlike state of dependency can happen for many reasons. Amongst people who have learning disabilities being like a child can be a means of protection from a rejecting world. The 'world's' collusion with the dynamics of infantilisation is culturally a means of avoiding pain as well. Sinason describes this when she writes about how anyone can be ignorant or not knowing and how avoiding knowledge protects us from unbearable loss

(Sinason 1992: 1). For a person who has a learning disability (or any disability), their journey into maturation can involve acknowledgement of how they are different from others, and this inevitably means a consideration of the loss inherent in the disability. For those who share their life the pain of acknowledging that loss can also be intolerable. The avoidance of the difference between the disabled self and non-disabled others can be about avoiding unbearable envy.

The environment of a person and the capacity of their family or carers for empathic nurturing are key to development. Parenting is a challenge to any parent and raising a child with a learning disability is, arguably, more so. The experience of having a child who is 'lacking' can be a wound to the ordinary expectations and fantasies of the parent. How a parent adjusts and copes with not being 'mirrored' by their child can affect the development of attachment. Adjustment to the loss that a disability inevitably means is a painful and complex task for parents, with lifelong implications. Guilt, anxiety, shame and anger are feelings that parents often describe and express. Ziolko (1991) talks about how the desire to avoid this pain, overcompensate and deny are usual and can be seen as a means of coping with the trauma.

The assessment and possible diagnosis of disability can be a highly stressful experience for parents who may have to deal with long periods of uncertainty. Parents can find themselves in the position of seeking out a diagnosis for their child which then has no remedying treatment, ultimately making them feel powerless and desperate. Much doubt and uncertainty exists. The task for parents is complex, and given that they are in a state of mourning for the loss of their 'normal child' (Kuczaj 1998: 154) trauma can affect their own resilience and capacity to think. Knowing how a diagnosis will impact their child's lifelong development is for most another uncertainty. Over-protection of the child is a common response from parents.

For parents of a child with a disability, rejection can appear to be all around. Their child may become the focus of a lot of medical attention with its emphasis at times on what is 'lacking'. Educationally, their child may be debated over extensively as authorities try to work out which provision is best. The norms of development may haunt them, with competitive and idealised images of 'perfect' children represented in the media. Faced with a rejecting gaze from society, parents who over-protect their disabled child can be doing this for very sane reasons.

My working context

I work in a Learning Disability Child and Adolescent Mental Health Service (LDCAMHS), whose aim is to support the mental well-being of infants, children, young people and their families. A lot of my work happens in a variety of special needs schools which generously allow me space and the privacy necessary for art psychotherapy sessions with children. I have access to therapy space in the health service owned property and this is sometimes utilised with patients who can be transported to sessions. I also provide psychotherapy/counselling informed sessions for parents/carers and sometimes do this concurrently whilst seeing the child in the

Plate 2.1 Patrick: Dracula.

Plate 2.2 Patrick: Scar.

Plate 3.1 Paul: 'Dad and the churchyard'.

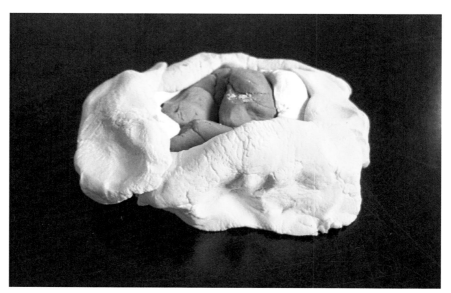

Plate 3.2 Paul: Model 1.

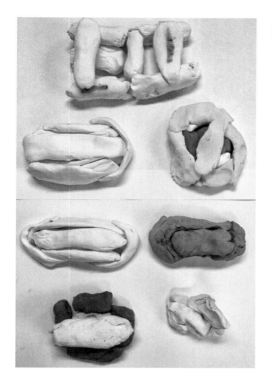

Plate 3.3 Various models made by Paul

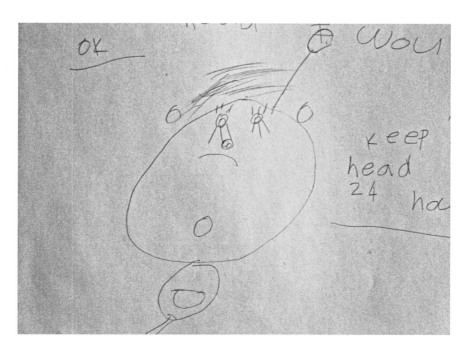

Plate 4.1 Leila: Shunt image detail.

Plate 5.1 Judy: Walking into the sea.

Plate 5.2 Ruth: Cat and kitten.

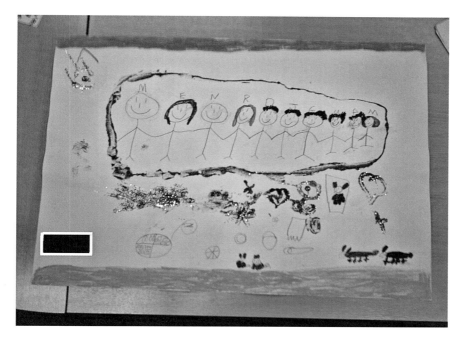

Plate 6.1 Catherine: Family group.

Plate 6.2 Catherine: Symbolic painting.

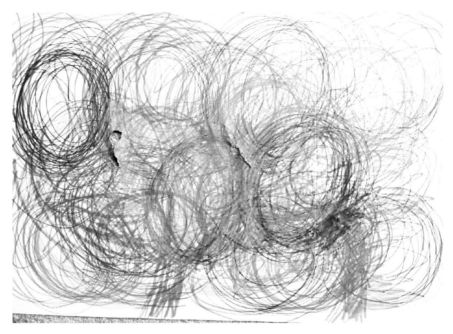

Plate 7.1 Tony: 'Me calm down'.

Plate 7.2 Cheryl: 'My house and friends'.

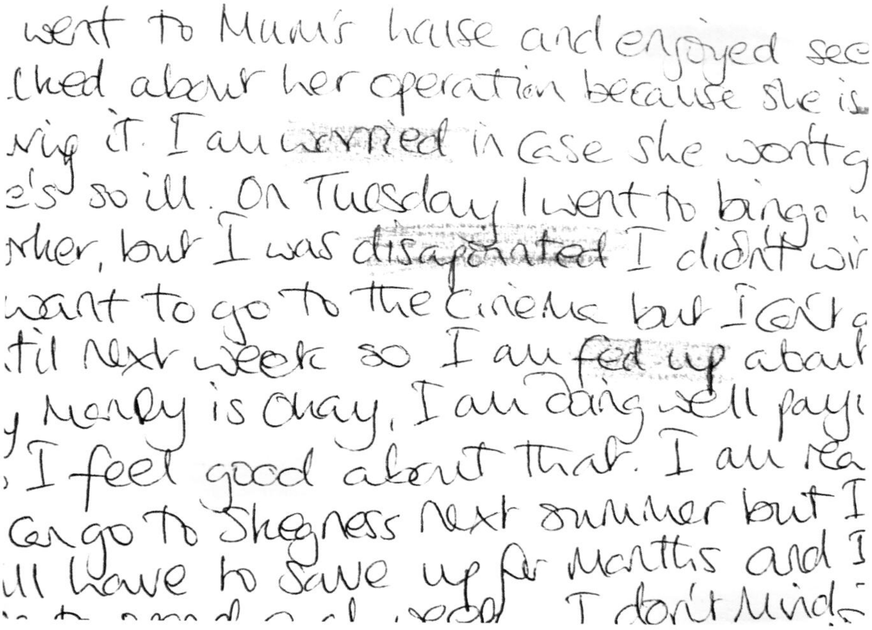

went to Mum's house and enjoyed see
ched about her operation because she is
ing it. I am worried in case she won't g
e's so ill. On Tuesday I went to bingo w
ther, but I was disapointed I didn't wi
want to go to the cinema but I can g
til next week so I am fed up about
y Mandy is okay, I am doing well payi
, I feel good about that. I am rea
can go to Skegness next summer but I
ll have to save up for months and I
is th a mand a al 1000 I don't mind.

Plate 7.3 Laura: 'Good and bad feelings' (diary entry).

Plate 8.1 Thomas: Pram.

Plate 9.1 David B: The Theatre.

Plate 9.2 David B: The Beast.

family for art psychotherapy sessions. Usually, families are seen by a number of professionals from the service; a particular psychology colleague has often seen the parents/carers whilst I have worked with the child. This isn't set in stone though and depending on need, different treatment plans are considered.

Catherine

In order to illustrate some aspects of the complexity that is infantilisation I would like to discuss Catherine, which isn't her real name but it is one she chose when I discussed this chapter with her. I saw her for sessions in her school and saw her mother for sessions concurrently, but less frequently. Catherine was referred for art psychotherapy assessment when she was 15 years old. The period of therapy lasted for approximately two-and-a-half years with a reducing frequency of sessions in the last year. Catherine is a young woman with a mild to moderate learning disability who has a diagnosis of autism. She was referred by her psychiatrist, the initial thoughts being that her very demanding behaviour with her mother may decrease if she were able to develop a trusting relationship with someone outside the family. She was particularly distressed at night, finding the letting go of her mother very difficult. Mum described how Catherine would call out to her once she was in bed asking repetitive questions. Mum would try to remain calm, answering the questions as the family went off to bed, but as things became quieter Catherine would become more distressed. The distress was considered to be mum's responsibility, other family members feeling that their input wouldn't be welcome or may even cause more distress. For Catherine it sounded like there was no means of comfort for the experience of being alone. The consequence was a sleep-deprived family. Catherine had an older brother at home along with her dad. Both men had retreated into isolative positions; they and mum were tiptoeing around a distressed and challenging Catherine.

Catherine was diagnosed with neurofibromatosis at age six. This is a physical condition in which the nerve tissue grows tumours that may be benign or may cause serious damage by compressing nerves and other tissues, the range of affect being quite mild in some people to severe in others. Cognitive impairment is common. It is a condition that requires monitoring as the affect on the brain and central nervous system can change throughout a person's life. There are risks that later adolescence and early adulthood can be a time of increased change and possibly more impairment. In Catherine's case the monitoring was inadequate and irregular – the national standards for monitoring is in effect variable and parents knew of other services in the country that provided more regular monitoring. The parents were worried that Catherine's behavioural challenges were the effect of changes in the status of the neurofibromas (tumours) in her brain; their fear was that progressive damage could be affecting her behaviourally. Their adjustment to the loss they knew of was impacted by the loss they feared in the future.

Catherine is the only daughter and youngest child in her family. She has two older brothers one of whom was still at home during the time of her art psychotherapy treatment. Mum worked from home and provided the majority of care in the family while dad described work as providing him with some relief from the stress of home life. Catherine dominated mum's attention when the family were together and other family members had grown to experience resentment and anger at Catherine. She was particularly challenging in her efforts to have mum all to herself. They spoke of feeling exhausted and exasperated.

I was able to work with Catherine in her school, an environment which was experienced by her as unempathetic, her need for individual attention being thwarted by the needs of other young people. She struggled to maintain relationships with peers whom she experienced as accepting and rejecting, oscillating between the two. She had a particular interest in a children's TV programme called *Best of Friends* in which groups of young friends conquered particular challenges in order to win prizes – teamwork was what made them successful; Catherine's desire to have a strong network of friends was clear. What happened, though, was that her real friendships at school didn't live up to the programme. Her idealisation of the TV programme was in some ways blocking the development of her venturing into a more mixed experience of real friendships. A repeating pattern was for her to return home from school and express the distress of her school day to her mum who in turn developed a view of school as cold and rejecting. Mum felt Catherine blamed her for what she experienced, which left her feeling helpless to change anything.

The development of friendships at special needs schools is something that I became more interested in. Whilst working with Catherine I began to see how the possibilities of friendship making were complicated. Pupils who attend special needs schools are usually drawn from a wider geographical area than mainstream schools – they rarely have peers at school who live in their local neighbourhood, which affects their access to each other out of school time. Class sizes are necessarily smaller and the school environment itself is a highly adult supervised place, making the establishment of friendships harder in some ways as there is less privacy and a smaller number of peers to draw from. Relationships are at times intense with a sense that everyone knows everyone else's business. Catherine had little contact with peers outside school, and her parents had little opportunity for developing relationships with other parents of young people at the school. The norm of seeing other parents at the school gates doesn't apply to many special needs schools as children are usually picked up from their homes in buses and transported to and from school. The casual contact that is generally seen as being conducive to relationship building is limited.

Catherine had developed a strong interest in collections and had amassed many dolls and soft toys. She spent happy hours collecting these toys and they filled her bedroom. In addition, collecting rubbish was something that Catherine did and not being able to throw rubbish away was an indicator to mum that Catherine's anxiety levels were increasing. She collected rubbish in bags and for a while sealed them up and put them under her bed; attempts by mum to throw them away caused distress. Another collection and interest was 'Hello Kitty' stationery and trinkets, a brand which is characterised by a girl figure that smiles blankly, appears ideally happy and is very cute. The trinkets are made with close attention to detail and are small. The volume of the collections excited Catherine; she knew their names but a further description of them was limited. The acquiring of them usually happened at weekends and mum described how Catherine expressed very little satisfaction about what she had. Catherine was in a constant state of desiring more. Parts of the collections were bundled each day into a number of bags and taken to school. They were sometimes taken out and shown to others but mostly they remained in the bags and were taken home again. Their power as what Winnicott termed 'transitional objects' is clear (Abram 1996: 343–347) as they did provide some soothing in the face of the anxiety-provoking transitions between home and school. The fact that there were so many of them and that they were mostly sealed in bags, in some ways ameliorated the effect as there was little sense of them actually being known. There was a sense that they were never enough and the collection kept being added to. If taken as an expression of Catherine's feelings related to separation, they suggested that perfection was idealised. As they were bundled up in small bags they were also partly denied and kept hidden.

Early sessions

In Catherine's first sessions the time available and the ending of the time were a great focus of her attention, suggestive of the attachment related difficulties she was experiencing. It was a very hopeful sign though that these feelings were voiced. Catherine initially sought much reassurance about her choices, even going so far as to ask me to make the choices for her which I resisted. She did choose to make an image which described her family and how she saw herself within it. No hierarchy appeared, all figures stood in a long line, the heights varied but facial expression didn't. Her descriptions of the family were in some ways similar to the lists of preferred dolls. However, Catherine did show me who was most significant to her, placing herself between her mum and 'nana' (see Plate 6.1). This image making led to descriptions of the relationship she had enjoyed with her nana whose death a few years previously had affected Catherine deeply. There is a sense in the drawing that by seeing all members of the family as very similar, difference is avoided and an idealised 'we are one' is created. In the image, Catherine included all her grandparents, although she had known only her nana. There is a sense in which past generations are important for her but perhaps this image again echoes a oneness.

Catherine made a shift into a more abstract image (see Plate 6.2) in which she describes herself and others in shapes and lines – she is surrounded by many crosses, or kisses, and the outer grid separates and protects. There is uncertainty about whether the crosses are either symbols of something being wrong or symbols of affection. It seems to me that this image was a turning point, as after it little art making took place and there was a focus on play and talking. Looking back on it, the image appears to describe the quality of protection that Catherine requires as she feels vulnerable and under attack.

Sessions with parents

Throughout Catherine's therapy separate sessions were provided for her parents as well – I provided sessions with her mum who used the time to consider her feelings of anxiety about Catherine and isolation. Mum's capacity to understand her daughter was enhanced by her own adolescent memories of isolation and loneliness. She had struggled in her separation from her parents, their need of her being an oppressive and guilt inducing experience. Catherine's image which included grandparents she hadn't known seemed to find an echo in what her mum was describing. Sessions with her dad were with a psychology colleague and were aimed at providing him with an opportunity to consider his isolated position. He struggled with the development of the relationship and chose to withdraw. It was evident that each member of the family was struggling with their own personal difficulties of stress and, at times, depression. Catherine's protests and challenging behaviour, particularly at night, could be seen as expressing the family's feelings as well as her own. It was through sessions with her mum that I understood more of the dilemma she faced in 'letting Catherine go'. What was outside the family felt unsafe and unprotected and what was inside the family, although protective, was at times angry and exasperated.

Bruce (undated) talks about how parents can benefit from being 'let off the hook of guilt' through professional support. This legitimises their own grief and trauma and helps them to understand how this can affect their feelings of attachment towards their child. Being listened to validates the complex tasks and feelings of over-protection that parents face. I hope I was able to offer Catherine's mum this support.

At various points throughout the therapy Catherine's mum made a conscious effort to make herself less available to her daughter. This took the form of going away on short breaks with her friends and slowly increasing the number of nights away as Catherine survived each experience. These were not easy times and they involved much discussion and exploration of the anxieties that were encountered. She also began to describe to Catherine more clearly how her behaviour affected her and what the impact was on other members of the family. Significantly, they all survived the experience and the separations became less feared and less mysterious.

Shops and exchange

Catherine was very engaging and as her confidence developed within the sessions she began to explore her feelings about relationships and her sense of understanding 'what makes people tick'. She arrived at this through the games and play she introduced. Catherine designed a shop till out of her art materials box and made pretend money. She used the many objects and trinkets that she carried to and from school each day and arranged them in a pretend shop in which she was either the customer or shopkeeper and I took the other role. This lively play was repeated over many sessions. I have warm memories of playing shop as a child and this play was very satisfying to us both. The variations and roles played out were diverse but it was clear that the shopkeeper role was her preferred part. Whilst this enabled her to exercise control she remained polite, and being a 'professional' shopkeeper was clearly an aspiration. In this she was negotiating the letting go of her prized toys and collection to me – a respectful buyer at times but also someone who was at other times greedy and bought everything and at times very selective and bought only a few things. The game structure allowed her to know that all objects would be returned and there developed an ever-expanding sense that our roles could be stretched. To me the game seemed like we were practising social roles, which sometimes involved tolerating disappointment and frustration. A typical session of 'shop' began with Catherine presenting and listing the contents of the shop after which we engaged in exchange where novelty and our views of the contents were shared. Catherine was 16 years old at this point and we were playing a game typical of much younger children but this play felt important to experience. Some of the ways in which she would talk echoed the list-like descriptions she used when, in earlier sessions, she had introduced me to her toy collections. The possibility of playing shop in the next session was something she expressed as being soothing, the sessions being a point of relief after a difficult week. During the shop game there emerged a pattern of discussing how relationships at school were affecting her and Catherine would discuss real disappointments. To this I would reflect her feelings, aiming to aid her exploration of what was a journey into the disillusionment of real friendships and fear of loneliness. What she allowed to develop was a more mature way of relating – she was trying to work out why people were behaving the way they were rather than blaming others or expecting that someone else would sort out the difficulty. Her interest in the children's TV programme *Best of Friends* waned and a new interest in the TV soap *Eastenders* emerged. In this programme, conflict is on the agenda in every episode, loss is acknowledged and any opportunity for a drama is sought out. The way in which Catherine could list the names of the roles remained and was coupled with an interest in the storylines but the expectation and ideal of *Best of Friends* was certainly different.

At times I encountered doubt about whether what we were engaged in was credible. Within supervision I considered that it was hard to know where we were headed. At times I felt very hopeful and then a conflict or disappointment occurred at school or with her siblings. It seemed as if Catherine was always going to be dependent on the relationship with her mum as a means to soothe her experiences in the wider world. The quality of reassurance Catherine required at the end of sessions, the desire to repeat the plans for the next session and the number of times she said goodbye felt as if the need wouldn't be met. The play was enjoyable but felt like it was part of the protected bubble in which idealised relating was being held onto. My enjoyment of the sessions in a way had me wondering who was being 'therapised'. Was my enjoyment a means of avoiding the pain of loneliness of which this work was stimulating my own memories? The enjoyment became mixed with guilty feelings as if enjoyment needed to be a burdened experience.

I had doubts about where the boundary lay between therapist and client. Again guilt was prominent. Although the sessions were non-directive and Catherine took the lead in choosing what was explored, had my own fears made me influence a rescue that in a way denied the existence of the loss? The therapist's role is not to protect the client from outer reality and it seemed that I was. It seemed that the expectations were too high in the therapy, that somehow the therapy would find the solution to Catherine's loneliness or even to her disability. Here I think I was experiencing some of the stress that Catherine's mum experienced and some of Catherine's own desire to deny her disability.

The ability to make friends and maintain friendship is based upon the capacity to be alone – 'in order to hold the friend in mind whilst also recognizing separateness' (Abram 1996: 349). Catherine has a diagnosis of autism from which one could draw an assumption that relating to others is going to be difficult as she struggles with understanding what others are experiencing. However, Catherine clearly had a desire to develop relationships and to understand consciously what was genuine and authentic about these relationships. Her experience of the more paranoid features of her doubts about peers and others and her desire to explore these had hopefulness in it that suggests she was moving through stages of development towards a more sure sense that being alone is tolerable. I was surprised at how capable she was. It threw up my own prejudices about what a person with a label of autism would be like.

Blaming the outer world to protect the inner world

I felt as if I was on a see-saw. I was deeply frustrated by an outer world whose 'fault' it was for Catherine's experience of isolation, while at other times I experienced Catherine as being the reason why the world withdrew from her. This in turn led to the rise of guilty feelings in me for attacking her. The experience of loneliness in adolescence is essential in Winnicottian theory:

> At adolescence when the individual is undergoing pubertal changes and is not quite ready to become one of the adult community there is a strengthening of the defences against being found, that is to say being found before being there to be found. That which is truly personal and which feels real must be defended at all cost, and even if this means a temporary blindness to the value of compromise.
>
> (Abram 1996: 100)

Trying to understand Catherine was hard, the confusion about whether this was an unknowable, essentially defended state; whether my difficulty in knowing her was about the difference between us, her having a learning disability and me not; or whether this was about the capacities of her learning ability. My confusion was mirroring her own I think. Feelings of paralysis haunted me. When confidence is low our capacity to stay certain about experiences falters, and we doubt what we think. I was in a state of 'mirroring' what I perceived to be the quality of attack Catherine experienced. It was interesting that her presentation and play was at times very much within the realm of a much younger child's play but the dilemmas that emerged were very much about the difficulties of an adolescent.

In therapy, regressive states are usual and are the realm within which more archaic self-objects are encountered and experienced within the therapeutic dyad (Kohut 1971: 7). However, with a client who has a learning disability there possibly is the desire to attack the regression as if it were yet another level of damage that this time the therapist is responsible for – as if regression to earlier stages of development needs to be avoided at all costs. When I considered what my manager or what the head teacher of the school might think if they were present in the session – a fly on the wall – images of humiliation and shame became prominent. If I was to transfer this experience of playful relating to a client who didn't have a disability I think I would more confidently see the health of the situation which in effect was what Catherine was bringing to the sessions – a healthy regressing, a revisiting of a developmental stage that had strengths that could be usefully employed.

As therapy progressed, there was a significant reduction in the frequency of distressed nights and, through careful supervision, an end date was agreed upon. Catherine could now tolerate her mother being away overnight and she made trips away with her school; some of which were satisfying and some of which were not. She voiced more of her needs in relationships and had begun to express dissatisfaction to the people who were directly involved. This was a developing skill. Changes had taken place for mum, too – there still remained a great sense of responsibility for her daughter but there was some resignation that disappointments were inevitable. Catherine could become calmer, through mum's capacity to hear her.

I think mum had allowed herself to feel that she didn't have to repair everything – this being beyond her abilities (and those of anyone else). The ending of therapy happened over a period of a year, the sessions decreasing in frequency and the ending becoming more and more a focus in the sessions. Reflections near the end of therapy covered what had been achieved and what hadn't. Catherine spoke of her desire that the sessions wouldn't end. She focused on the comfort the sessions had provided, the quality of attention and listening she had received. Like other separations this one has been distressing but also has been survived.

So what is infantilisation?

A parent can quite ordinarily experience feeling blamed by their child as they begin to experience the disappointments of the 'real' world. Parents of babies or infants are ordinarily haunted by quite catastrophic thoughts about what might happen to their child if their protection fails – although this is distressing it is necessary as it means that parents do what they can to provide that constant protection. A quality of infantilisation can be seen as an eternal state where parents feel that their child is as vulnerable as the day they were born. Acknowledgement that the child has developed is denied in some ways because, possibly, the catastrophe of the disability has happened and they are overshadowed by guilt. That position of isolation further exacerbates the persecutory feelings and the prison walls are drawn. The 'being let off the hook of guilt' is obviously what is needed but, for some parents, the grief is so complex as to make that seem impossible. There is a sense of the grieving process being frozen; fears about the past, present and future are overwhelming and traumatising. Soothing those anxieties can become out of reach.

In therapy, Catherine allowed some of her capacities to be seen or found – I think she surprised herself (and me) with some of her insights. She allowed herself to lead the way into play and games which developed her trust in me – I think she knew I was going to enjoy playing shop. She wanted to be genuinely liked and achieved this. Her capacity for doing this comes from her experience of being lovingly parented and played with – memories which she didn't deny. Approaching the facts of her disability was clearly very painful for her and she avoided any suggestion I made to discuss this. Hopefully, Catherine's experience of art therapy has provided her with a solid foundation from which she will continue to explore, develop and mature.

References

Abram, J. (1996). *The Language of Winnicott: A Dictionary of Winnicott's Use of Words*. London: Karnac Books.

Bruce, E. (undated).'Mother, Father, Siblings and Children Adapting to Disability'. Vicnet (State library of Victoria, Australia), sourced from the internet: home.vicnet.net.au/~ejbruce/elite.htm (accessed 1 February 2011).

Kohut, H. (1971). *The Analysis of the Self: A Systematic Approach to the Psychoanalytic Treatment of Narcissistic Personality Disorders*. Chicago: University of Chicago Press.

Kuczaj, E. (1998). 'Learning to Say "Goodbye"', in M. Rees (ed.) *Drawing on Difference*. London: Routledge.

Sinason, V. (1992). *Mental Handicap and the Human Condition: New Approaches from the Tavistock*. London: Free Association Books.

Ziolko, M. (1991). 'Counselling Parents of Children with Disabilities: A Review of the Literature and Implications for Practice', *Journal of Rehabilitation* April–June issue.

Part V

Fear

Talking about fear and anxiety

Jo

I was quite angry . . . didn't believe in the world . . . thought the world was against me . . . was getting into a lot of trouble . . . anxiety was really high . . . possibly feeling worthless.

I had um bad voices . . . they were telling me all sorts of things and um not to do anything good, just bad stuff. I didn't know whether to take it or not but they were dominating me to do bad stuff and I got into a bit of a knife crime . . . Like going to the surgery and that . . . threatened to kill myself and um I ended up getting taken away . . . went to um the police station . . . and was taken to court the next day.

Just tried to work out what made me do it and things like that rather than keeping it back and not moving forward . . . drew it and wrote things down . . . what the voices were telling me to do and working it out step by step . . . what happened and what went wrong and realised that wasn't my normal self to have done that, it's just the voices at the time were crowding me.

When I first saw the voices and heard them and they were following me and stuff, I actually drew the image of what it looked like and how many of them there were, like the black figure . . . of the voice there . . . and got like the black pool and the blue pool and then the red pool . . . a bit like lava from a volcanic eruption. They were just combined together really and it shows just how much I wanted the voices to go . . . and I managed to um battle them myself and get them out . . . because voices aren't very pleasant and it does crowd your life . . . takes over you.

Chapter 7

'The long fingers of fear'

Elizabeth Ashby

Twenty minutes ago an incident occurred when Steve, a tall well-built 40-year-old man with a severe learning disability and autism, lashed out at two support workers. Another day centre member called Cindy also caught the brunt of his anger as he rushed past pushing her out of his way. The two support workers, who were winded and bruised but otherwise unhurt, rushed to her aid but she had already become very distressed and had slumped to the floor, moaning. Another two support workers overtook their colleagues and restrained Steve before he assaulted anyone else and supported him to go to the sensory room to calm down. The setting is a unit for twelve people with severe learning disabilities who also have autism; fortunately only five are in the unit at this time. Each of those individuals reacts in very different ways.

I am in the art therapy room preparing for a session with Tony. Tony is angrily pacing about in the lobby of the unit, aggressively thrusting his face close to the faces of staff members, asking tersely 'Where's Li[z]?' They step back, looking threatened, and tell him he has to wait for five minutes for his session. To his right, slumped against the wall on the floor is Cindy, who is refusing to get up from the floor and periodically hitting her head with her fist and banging it against the wall, moaning. This seems to make all the staff feel deskilled and demoralised – they have not been able to stop her.

Joe is opening and shutting the door of the music room with a bang over and over again as he rocks from one foot to the other. Henry is in the lounge hiding in a corner waving his fist at people and muttering, and Suzy is running up and down the corridor, leaping and shouting and threatening to hit everyone she passes (but doesn't) – it seems that part of her is enjoying the chaos, but part of her is afraid. The staff are working hard at not showing their anxiety and trying to bestow calm on the situation, but the mood is catching. The people with learning disabilities who are in the building, particularly Cindy, are very agitated and upset, and I am apprehensive about the session I am due to have with Tony. I wonder whether to cancel it.

Bob, Tony's support worker, comes up to me when I emerge from the room, dodging Suzy and Cindy, and says he will sit outside the room in case I need help during the session and I also have a personal alarm on my belt. I walk to the middle of the lobby and say 'Hello Tony' keeping my voice as steady as I can, though my hands are a bit sweaty and my pulse has quickened. He turns from where he has been standing looking out of the window and looks at me, frowning. Tony does a little bending movement while waving his arms in front of him (not a good sign as it tends to precede aggressive behaviour) and charges off down the corridor towards my room. Bob and I follow as fast as we can.

I enter the art therapy room and see that Tony has sat down in his usual seat surrounded by the art materials I laid out for him. He has started to draw large circles frenetically on the paper, pressing so hard on the pens that the nibs bend and he makes holes in the paper. I cautiously sit to his left, nearest the door in case I need to get out fast, and wait quietly, not moving and hardly breathing, while he draws. Gradually, my anxiety recedes as Tony's mood softens while he rapidly draws on several sheets of paper, speaking occasionally. After about ten minutes he is calm, and he stops and looks at me, smiles, and says 'Loo[k]!', pointing at his work. Inwardly I sigh with relief and my body relaxes. As the session continues the atmosphere in the room becomes more comfortable; Tony is more communicative, and his drawing has slowed down and he has become more thoughtful (see Plate 7.1).

Aims of this chapter

This chapter is about fear and about how some people with learning disabilities whom I have worked with in art therapy have experienced it in their lives. The people I discuss in this chapter have been described as having mild (Laura), moderate (Cheryl) and severe (Tony) learning disabilities, in addition to mental health issues and/or autistic traits. I aim to demonstrate how their fear was expressed and how difficult it can be to identify fear sometimes as it may be masked by other emotions such as anger. I also discuss how therapists themselves may experience fear in the context of their work. I have called the chapter 'The Long Fingers of Fear' in an attempt to express something of the pervasive and intrusive quality of fear as well as its nature and presence in people's lives.

Before I discuss the opening vignette, I consider theory that I have found helpful when thinking about fear and how it affects people who have learning disabilities. First I explore ideas concerning anxiety, fear and terror, and then I discuss unconscious processes that people employ such as projective identification and splitting. I go on to identify sources of fear for people with learning disabilities, such as difficulties with communication, thinking and understanding. I demonstrate how fear operates on different levels, from individuals, to family members then families, communities and countries, and give some examples of how these fears impact on people who have learning disabilities.

I discuss some of my art therapy sessions with Tony and look at how fear was responded to by people with severe learning disabilities, further exploring the opening vignette, and going on to consider fear experienced by therapists; then I describe art therapy with Cheryl (who has a moderate learning disability); and finally with Laura (who has a mild learning disability), showing how fear was expressed and how it was addressed. The chapter concludes with a discussion of the issues presented. Pseudonyms have been used throughout this chapter and biographical details changed to protect people's identity. Throughout the chapter I hope to show how fear extends into society, and how important it is that art therapists are able to work with and recognise fear underlying other issues that people present.

Anxiety, fear and terror

For many people with learning disabilities that I have worked with, everyday experiences can hold both anxiety and fear. In psychoanalytic theory *anxiety* is the word used to describe feelings without a clear object, whereas *fear* is used when a clear object has been identified as the source of the feeling. However, everyday use of the words suggests that *fear* alludes to more powerful feelings than those described as *anxiety* (Wood 1997). Wood wrote about fear in the context of her work with people who have a history of psychosis, and noted that little had been written from a psychological perspective about fear with 'direct and sobering consequences for clients and practitioners alike' (ibid.: 41). She believed that people needed to know that their therapists had understood the sense of *terror* (my italics) that pervaded their experience of psychosis. Also, she thought that

> the way the therapeutic container is conceptualised is particularly vital in work where art therapists find themselves working with seriously deprived clients; a part of whose deprivation has been caused by serious obstacles to their ability to make sense of experience.
>
> (Ibid.: 43)

The 'primitive quality in the anxieties experienced by people with a history of psychosis' could be compared to 'early infant fears of death and annihilation' giving 'an indication of the extent of the terror that may be present in an adult in the midst of psychosis' (ibid.). Tustin described the experience of autistic children in similar terms in that 'behind such children's seeming lack of fear, there is a terror so great that it cannot be expressed' which needs to be put into words by the therapist, who must support the child in experiencing it (Tustin 1992: 123). Tustin considered that Bion's term 'nameless dread' appropriately described the experience of psychosis in autistic states which gives rise to acute terror, and which causes the development of an encapsulated autistic state in which a hard exterior protects a soft and vulnerable 'me'. The child lacks the apparatus to process the primitive impulses s/he feels, and has no capacity for dreaming – indeed the 'primordial stuff of dreams is his waking reality' and what is often felt is a 'tumult of rage, terror and excitement' (ibid.: 159).

For some people with learning disabilities (depending on the severity of learning disability) there can be a significant deficit in their capacity to make sense of their experience of life. This can result in general *anxiety* and confusion, and *fear* associated with abusive memories. Further, *terror* may be felt by people who are experiencing autistic states and/or psychosis in addition to their learning disability, or who have been exposed to particularly terrifying experiences. It is difficult to explore fear in isolation from other emotions that are present, as Tustin described above, and Wood suggested that therapists who have difficulty hearing the extent of the terror experienced by the person may avoid working with it (Wood 1997: 41). A cycle is likely in which confusion leads to anxiety or fear, and the consequent attack on thinking that the person experiences leads to more fear being experienced, and so on.

Unconscious processes

Problems with communication are often experienced by people who have learning disabilities, and projective identification is an unconscious form of communication that art therapists are likely to encounter in their work with people of all capacities, with or without a learning disability. It has been considered to be a particularly valuable form of counter-transference 'since the client or patient may transmit directly to the therapist the actual experience that he cannot manage' (Gomez 1997: 39).

The process of projective identification involves the person projecting feelings into the therapist who then experiences these feelings as their own, even acting in accordance with them; it is a powerful non-verbal form of communication (ibid.: 39). When this occurs between a baby and its mother, a successful outcome is determined by the mother's capacity to process the projection and reintroject it into the child. Through projective identification the therapist's counter-transference becomes very informative of the person's inner experience and, therefore, clinical supervision is particularly important to enable therapists to unravel the projection they are identifying with. A good example of this experience in practice was described by Schaverien (2007) who described an experienced art therapist supervisee acting as though under a spell which was broken in supervision by bringing the situation to consciousness, but not before the therapist had acted out some difficult behaviour under its influence.

My own experience of projective identification with people who have severe learning disabilities has led to counter-transference feelings of anxiety and fear, as well as frustration and anger, feeling deskilled and difficulty in thinking. A particularly difficult counter-transference feeling to cope with is one of deadness, which manifests itself as boredom, feeling stuck, apathy . . . and seems to roll itself out like a nihilistic blanket over the struggling therapist. Rees (1998) described this counter-transference as commonly experienced by art therapists she supervised, 'a feeling of suffocation or drowning' which she thought expressed the person's feeling of deadness or a death wish. Again, Bion's concept of 'nameless dread' ([1967] 1993) which leaves the person feeling that they are in a meaningless and mysterious world they cannot understand was identified as an appropriate description, a feeling that I am sure some of the people referred to me for art therapy would certainly have identified with.

Splitting is another unconscious process that many people with learning disabilities employ, as I will discuss in my vignettes. Splitting is a concept developed by Klein in which the child experiences bad internal objects as terrifying, and attempts to keep images of the good and bad objects apart; the child fears the bad objects and his/her own destructiveness. The more terrifying the child's fantasies are the more the child feels compelled to keep them apart; however, it is impossible for the child not to introject bad objects (Segal 1988a).

If splitting is not excessive (in which case rigidity may develop) it can be an important early defence which lays the foundations for less primitive forms of defence such as repression in later life. Splitting is associated with persecutory anxiety and idealisation, and though it continues to be experienced in adulthood it is to a far lesser extent if normal development takes place; if not, splitting distorts the adult's judgement. A small degree of persecutory anxiety enables adults to sense danger and react appropriately, and idealisation assists the development of a belief in goodness in others, and as such is the foundation of good object relations (ibid.).

Within my discussion of art therapy sessions with Cheryl and Laura I describe the splitting that I felt was employed by both of them, and go on to consider how people of all capacities can engage in splitting to some degree. It is more difficult to know whether splitting is taking place with people who have severe learning disabilities and little or no speech, though the lack of speech suggests a level of under-development, and therefore increases the likelihood of splitting.

Difficulties with communication, understanding and thinking

Many people who have learning disabilities also have difficulties with communication, understanding their experiences of life, and thinking about them. It is important to acknowledge that for each individual, these experiences vary considerably in their presentation. When working with people with learning disabilities the therapist may also experience, through the counter-transference, an attack on his/her capacity to think about the work; Sinason discussed her inability to think and her fear in the context of a session with a violent boy (Sinason 1992: 118). Good clinical supervision is necessary to combat the impact of the attack on thinking for therapists, and I have also found thinking together with colleagues helpful. As this is a common experience for therapists working with people with learning disabilities, I am surprised to find this so little discussed in the literature.

The process of the development towards communicating, understanding and thinking are remarkably complex, and include the capacity to symbolise, to develop a theory of mind, to dream, to express felt sensations as verbal thoughts, and so on. Bion's theory of thinking was dependant on two developmental processes, firstly the development of thoughts, and secondly the development of the apparatus to cope with them (thinking). Thoughts, he postulated, developed from pre-conceptions to conceptions or thoughts, and then to concepts (which are named and become fixed conceptions/thoughts). When a pre-conception (an 'empty' thought) comes into contact with a 'realisation' the result is a conception; the infant's capacity to tolerate frustration further develops the capacity for thinking, but if under-developed leads to disturbed thought processes (Bion 1993: 110–112).

Symbolisation was considered by Segal to be crucial to the development of speech, since the capacity to form symbols is fundamental to verbal thought and thereby to the use of words. This is an internal process which underpins the capacity to be aware of one's unconscious, and is necessary for external communication (Segal 1988b: 165). Disturbances in the development of these capacities are also responsible to a large extent for the difficulties people experience with communication. Many people with learning disabilities think in concrete terms, some, such as Cindy, having little capacity to symbolise (which results in lack of speech and pre-representational image making such as scribbling). Some have the potential to develop symbolisation (Tony had a few words and showed some developmental progress), and some have an ability to symbolise but no capacity for abstract thought (which was Cheryl's experience).

Babies who have not been adequately nurtured by a thinking and feeling 'mother' experience her absence as persecutory and unbearable; fearful feelings result. It is difficult for the child to understand such concepts as thinking and feeling if no one is doing this for them (Sinason 1992: 189). Attachment difficulties result, and the child who has received none of the necessary prerequisites for normal development will grow up to experience difficulties with symbol and language development. Sinason also showed how children who had no physical disability affecting their intelligence could be handicapped by abuse by their primary caregivers (ibid.).

When a person with a learning disability experiences some, or all, of these difficulties affecting their thinking and communication, the disabling impact affects all aspects of the person's daily life and consequently is a source of anxiety and fear as s/he struggles to understand.

Other sources of fear

Fear and anxiety can be far-reaching and experienced on different relational levels. Individual experiences of these emotions exist on one level, between family members (as in the case of one abusing another), and within families fear and anxiety can be felt towards others outside the family unit who are perceived as a threat. Communities representing racial or religious groups, or those who are somehow seen as different and therefore unacceptable, may experience interference, intimidation and violence from those who oppose them. Ultimately, countries and continents experience these same problems at even further horrific levels and with even greater consequences.

De Groef discussed attitudes towards people with learning disabilities as a 'dark continent', in which disgust at the handicapped infant and shame at the failure to produce a normal child prevail (De Groef 1999; Sinason 1992), and fear of contagion resulted in abusive attempts to hide and restrain people who were thought to be mad or developmentally disabled. Several older people in the unit where I worked with Tony had been incarcerated as children in large impersonal institutions where their care was less than humane, only being rehabilitated into the community many years later as a result of the Community Care Act (1990).

A significant number of individuals with learning disabilities also experience physical problems which may be related to a genetic disorder, or in some cases the result of an accident. Epilepsy is particularly prevalent among people with learning disorders. There are several types of epilepsy leading to different types of seizures, some of which can be very unpleasant for the sufferer, causing violent involuntary body movements and interfering with brain function, sometimes resulting in injury. Some people know when a seizure is likely, and others experience them with no warning. Seizures can be very frightening and seriously incapacitating.

Fear is experienced both consciously and unconsciously. When challenging behaviour has taken place, fear is the emotion least likely to be discussed in terms of the person's response to events, while frustration and anger are generally more evident. Although unrecognised perhaps by both the challenging individual and those around them, because it is felt bodily first and then cognitively, reactions to fear can be varied and misunderstood. Much challenging behaviour, as we saw from the vignette, stems from fear in situations, though each person responded in different ways. Yet my experience has been that those who appear most aggressive are often as fearful themselves – turning their fear into anger seems to help them to feel more in control and able to respond, which is preferable to being overwhelmed, just as obsessive and self-harming behaviours appear to have similar results.

Hate crime and living in fear

Sadly, most people with learning disabilities I have worked with have experienced abuse of some kind during the course of their lives – physical, sexual, emotional/psychological, neglect, financial, racial, institutional and discriminatory – and these abusive experiences have been a source of much fear and anxiety, perhaps even terror. While it is important that people with learning disabilities are able to lead good quality lives, are given choices and are allowed to make important decisions, even unwise ones (as discussed more fully in Chapter 1), the following events show how vulnerable people with learning disabilities can be, both in the community and at home.

Shockingly, I experienced the untimely death of two people I worked with. Charlie was a man with a moderate learning disability in his forties, who lived in a residential group home supported by a staff team; he was fairly independent and travelled around the local area unassisted. However, he was extremely traumatised by events in his past, and was lonely and consequently vulnerable to offers of friendship from dubious characters. One day Charlie disappeared without trace, and all those who worked with him feared for his safety while they waited for news from the police. Months later his body was found in a river several miles away. Nobody knows what happened in the intervening time.

The second person was Margaret, who had been experiencing difficulties with her carers which had been a considerable source of anxiety and fear for her; she distrusted them, suspected them of financial abuse and was not happy with their management of her daily affairs. However, she felt powerless to act on her fears and have the carers replaced, and had no family to represent or protect her. She was a wheelchair user and needed an important operation that would improve her quality of life which was a complex procedure, a source of hope but also fear. When it took place after a long wait, the skilled operation was successful and Margaret was expected to make a good recovery and thrive after her convalescence; in hospital she made good progress, but when she returned home her health began to fail and she died suddenly. It was thought her death was the result of neglect by her carers.

Charlie's death illustrates the vulnerability of the person with a learning disability when out in the community, while Margaret's death illustrates the possible abuse a person with a learning disability may experience even within their own home.

Art therapy with Tony

Returning to the opening vignette I will say more about my work with Tony and the other people in the day centre. Tony was a healthy, strong, ambulant young man with a severe learning disability and autism; he had little speech, understood only simple sentences, and spoke of himself in the third person, not having quite grasped the concept of 'I/ me'. Reports of his childhood contained accounts of neglect, fear and abuse while in the care of his birth mother and he was taken into foster care by the age of ten. Tony had been having art therapy sessions with me for a year at the time of the incident. During this time, while I was in the art therapy room preparing for his session, he would bang impatiently on the door, then run out into the garden and bang on the windows, back and forth, until I was ready to begin the session. At first I found this behaviour quite alarming and was apprehensive as we began work together, unsure how the sessions would unfold. As the sessions progressed, however, I was more able to understand Tony's limited vocabulary, and read his moods, body language and behaviour.

Agitation and fear had been palpable within the building leading up to, and following, the incident, and Tony was in a potentially aggressive state as he began his session. I knew, however, that he responded well to the soothing nature of drawing in the quiet facilitating atmosphere of the art therapy room and by offering such containment I was able to diffuse the tension in him. The opening vignette demonstrated how fear spread throughout the unit to each individual following the incident, resulting in an increase of challenging behaviour, which increased the fear the staff experienced too. The cycle is perpetuated and intensifies if it is not interrupted, as it was for Tony by starting his art therapy session in a safe and containing space away from the chaos.

Fear reached a crescendo when all the people in the day centre were reacting in different ways to their fear of being attacked. Cindy, who had Down's syndrome but no speech, had become very agitated as she had been pushed out of the way so hard; she had reacted in a familiar manner, slumped on the floor and self-harming by hitting her head with her hand and banging her head against the wall (perhaps trying to knock fearful thoughts out). Henry, a much older member of the unit whose speech resembled confusing riddles, had withdrawn into his favourite spot in a corner of the lounge where he stood defensively, half-turned towards the wall (seeking its protection), muttering angrily.

Joe had Fragile-X syndrome and was unable to speak but vocalised loudly, and obsessively and noisily banged a door over and over again; having control over this activity, even though it annoyed everyone, seemed to help him overcome his fear. Suzy became over-stimulated and reacted aggressively by threatening to hit people (which she did sometimes) and leapt around shouting; this behaviour further intensified the fear experienced by everyone in the centre including the staff. As we saw, Tony also reacted aggressively but was experienced as more menacing in the way he expressed his angry response than Suzy, perhaps because of his size; it seemed that angry feelings were easier to tolerate than the very primitive feelings of fear Tony first experienced within his body before his mind caught up with what was happening.

Through his art therapy sessions, over a period of three years, Tony developed a greater capacity to contain his frustration and to delay gratification. He could use art materials to help him think at some fundamental level and to soothe himself when agitated (thus reducing his aggression to some extent). Most of his image making was pre-representational (like the drawing in Plate 7.1), but he was able to use stencils to symbolise some ideas he wanted to communicate. I found that a tremendously high level of fear, frustration, anger, exhaustion and feeling of being deskilled, in addition to an attack on my thought processes, was being projected into me on a daily basis (and this seemed true for all the staff). I also experienced the nihilistic counter-transference in every session, and came to dread it. However, despite these difficulties, Tony came to greatly value the therapeutic relationship, and the length of time it continued allowed him much-needed time to develop, which he could only do very slowly. It also gave him a sense of continuity which was needed due to the rapid and cumulative experience of loss felt when valued support workers left the unit.

Therapists' fear

Before I go on to discuss the next two vignettes, I feel it is important to say something about the fear that the therapists, including myself, and other support workers experience when working with people with severe learning disabilities and challenging behaviour. Fear is experienced by the staff every day they enter the unit. This fear is a result of working with people who express what they cannot speak about by using their bodies as a form of communication; people who can be unpredictable, chaotic and volatile at times, depending on events which might trigger such behaviour. The staff, including art therapists, experience the very real possibility of being injured at work (which many are), being exposed to abusive language and bodily substances, and of witnessing clients' self injury, which they may not be able to prevent. In addition, when management is not available to support the staff during incidents, a great deal of responsibility rests on the workers in terms of carrying out procedures designed to reduce risk, attempting to protect the challenging person and other people in the vicinity, including other workers.

In her paper on art therapy-based organisational consultancy, Huet (2011) discussed work she did with members of the staff team of a secure unit for people with learning disabilities; in particular, she explored the emotional impact of working in such an environment where challenging behaviour is a day-to-day occurrence. Huet cited Foster (2001) who says that:

> the duty to care for the most damaged and demanding clients in society puts an expectation on staff in helping professions to be emotionally in touch with their clients' feelings. However, this means also being close to disturbing behaviour and to clients who often react against the closeness of the staff's involvement, and attack the care and/or the staff who deliver it.
>
> (Huet 2011:12)

Huet also addressed ways that staff members managed their difficult feelings, some presenting themselves as being 'immune to fear' and to 'almost welcome the challenge', while fear remained largely unacknowledged.

I myself have experienced several incidents in which a person grabbed my hair and shook me about. Other staff rushed to my aid and held the person's hands as still as possible, but encouraging him to release his grip took time. This type of assault does not sound dangerous but can result in serious head injury for the victim, though fortunately, in my case, I only experienced bruising and a headache. All my colleagues had, at some point, faced injuries such as being scratched, kicked or bitten. They have managed to remain professional in their responses and to continue to work with people despite the knowledge that they could be hurt. Risk management is an important part of such work, as are strategies such as personal alarms and response teams, and working without such precautions in this setting (which is not a forensic unit) is unwise.

Few art therapists have written about their personal experience of the issues I have been describing here, though Tipple (1992) has described working with a man on the ward until his aggressive behaviour diminished and they could move to the art therapy studio, and Hallam (1984) described a far from conventional collaborative approach to work with a very destructive person which involved him staying in the room and surviving the individual's attempts to destroy furniture and other destructive acts. Sinason (1992) described her fear in the presence of children and adolescents who engaged in violent behaviour towards themselves and others; she explored the impact of her fear on her thought processes and the practical measures she took to protect herself.

Despite these sobering experiences, the staff team I was part of were very committed to their work with the people who attended the unit, and were able to demonstrate that a therapeutic approach to their care over time did result in very different behaviour and a better quality of life.

Cheryl's experience of art therapy

For some people who have a learning disability, everyday activities can be a source of anxiety. This is often because the skills required to manage these activities are only partially available to them due to their cognitive and/or physical limitations. As a result, activities that people in the typically developed population take for granted, are difficult and anxiety-provoking: Cheryl was a person for whom this was true.

Cheryl, aged 35, had a moderate learning disability and was referred for art therapy because her carers were struggling with her challenging behaviour, which included refusal to co-operate with requests and hitting out periodically. In her home environment, it was reported that Cheryl experienced a volatile and chaotic upbringing which exposed her to domestic violence, drunkenness and neglect; she had no family connections since the death of a sibling some years earlier. Cheryl lived in a group residential home with several other people and a number of carers whom she mostly got on well with. She spent two years in individual art therapy and then joined a group for a further year-and-a-half. The setting for her therapy was an art therapy studio within a psychology department.

Cheryl seemed to understand more of what was said to her than she could express in words. She could sign her own name and write letters if words were spelled out to her, but seemed very uncertain of herself and her understanding of the world. A constant anxiety pervaded her interactions though, as she got to know me, she relaxed for short periods of time, taking encouragement from her perception of my understanding of her.

Life was experienced by Cheryl in concrete terms and in the here-and-now, which meant that, in therapy, she could only discuss issues that were currently of concern to her. Thus, she could not access events related to her childhood and remained closed off from those memories, though I suspect that events in her present experience from time to time stirred those memories and resulted in challenging behaviour.

Everyday activities were difficult for Cheryl because she could not tell the time, count money or read, and she struggled to understand much of what was said to her, hence her constant anxiety. These were the issues she brought to therapy but her images did not reflect the concerns she talked about – it seemed as though she was splitting. Some of the time the counter-transference had the nihilistic quality through her projective identification, and often it felt painful to me. Her verbal interaction concentrated on the events that caused her fear and anger (such as when she encountered youths on the top floor of the bus who intimidated and verbally abused her); at the same time she drew idealised scenarios showing herself and others in a happy time and place (often her home, on a bus, or on a walk in a park) (see Plate 7.2). I felt that this splitting was a necessary defence that she used against a frightening world and she could not develop beyond it.

Cheryl never drew any of the difficulties she experienced, though there were many. She gained confidence through her therapy despite maintaining the split between verbal discussion of the fears and anxieties which pervaded her life and her idealised happy images. It seemed to me that the splitting had the quality of a talisman, as if keeping them separate would make her life better in some magical way. However, I also think that her images were an expression of the 'handicapped smile' phenomenon that Sinason (1992) discussed and, as such, were an attempt to please me, and perhaps to protect me from her painful feelings. Following this course of art therapy, Cheryl's behaviour became far less challenging and my liaison with her staff enabled them to understand better how to manage her feelings, particularly when she was feeling upset.

Laura's art therapy

Laura was a young woman with a mild learning disability who was referred for art therapy as she was moving back into the community, having spent some time in a forensic unit because of dangerous fire-setting behaviours. Laura's home situation had been very volatile; she did not feel safe at home due to the chaotic way her mother dealt with household matters and relationships, and she was ill-prepared for life as an adult.

Her world was full of anxiety, and one day she set the lounge curtains on fire in response to an angry exchange with her mother during the day. The fire was quickly put out, but she became fascinated with the power she felt when playing with fire and experimented with lighting fires on waste ground when upset, angry and fearful. The situation at home was becoming more and more anxiety-provoking as it began to break down, and Laura was afraid. She set the house on fire again and consequently was detained for treatment under the Mental Health Act (1983).

Laura's chief difficulties, it transpired, were her inability to tolerate or acknowledge negative feelings, making connections between her emotions and behaviour, and lack of an emotional vocabulary. Laura had the potential to live independently in the community, and could effectively read, write and communicate verbally but was vulnerable because she understood less than seemed apparent. Laura eventually moved from the forensic unit to live in a house with staff who initially monitored her activities twenty-four hours a day. In time, they were able to be more supportive and taught her basic household management skills which she had not gained from education or her upbringing.

During her time in the forensic unit Laura had input from the psychology department which involved keeping a diary of specific behaviours, but she had not been able to think about them. Laura was very able creatively and enjoyed image making. She was clearly emotionally intelligent. Interestingly, like Cheryl, although she enjoyed drawing, painting and making three-dimensional objects, her subjects were always idealised and unconnected to the feelings she was able to describe verbally. I felt that she too engaged in splitting to a large extent.

The transformative work she achieved in therapy happened on many levels but was most clearly observable through her diary writing. She wrote specifically about how she felt about her experiences during the past week and, with encouragement, her writing became more creative and expressive, no longer limited by the rigidity that had previously been imposed on her. Each week, Laura read to me what she had written but, after a while, I realised that no negative feelings were being described. It seemed to me that her splitting, although not apparent in verbal communication, was present in her writing as well as her images.

One image she made was a 'feelings chart'; it was very large, free-standing and consisted of pieces of red and green card, and each week it was taken out and added to carefully. Laura wrote all the feeling words she could think of in attractive bubbles, putting the 'bad' feelings on the red side of the chart, and the 'good' feelings on the green side. She found the negative emotions far more difficult to identify than the positive ones, and as the weeks progressed her positive emotional vocabulary showed far more sophistication than the negative but, in time, this equalled out. This chart helped her develop a considerably expanded emotional vocabulary and formed a sort of backdrop to her sessions.

The split that was evident in her writing continued for some time, despite her increased vocabulary, as if there were no negative feelings in her life. I began to realise how scared (perhaps terrified) she was to acknowledge these difficult feelings, fearing they would totally overwhelm her (as they had done when she was fire-setting) and that naming them would give them too much power over her. In time Laura was able to acknowledge one or two negative emotions on the reverse of the page on which she had written her 'good' feelings. She seemed to equate her concept of 'good' and 'bad' feelings with 'good' and 'bad' parts of herself, and she greatly feared being seen as bad (she might get locked up again). However, she had been progressing well in her supported housing, and after a year the staff support was reduced so that she had a small measure of time alone in her home.

As her life gradually improved her fears subsided to some degree and she was more able to show how 'good' she could be. Her self-confidence increased and she began to feel she could risk acknowledging her 'bad' feelings more and we started a long process of gradually incorporating the bad with the good. A page of good feelings came easily to her, and then more reluctantly she was able to identify some bad feelings. Gradually her capacity to tolerate, identify and acknowledge the bad feelings increased and correspondingly the splitting seemed to decrease. As her splitting decreased, the transference feelings that interfered with my thinking about the work also eased, and I felt more energy in the sessions as time went on.

After about two years she was able to write a page that described both her good and bad experiences and her journey towards integration was gaining momentum.

The extract illustrated in Plate 7.3 shows the integration of the good feelings (coloured yellow) and bad feelings (in red), and the level to which her anxiety had receded much of the time (in her one reference to being worried). As Laura's fears gradually subsided she began to enjoy her growing independence, and was able to recognise areas of difficulty and plan coping strategies to manage her feelings.

Although Laura achieved so much through her art therapy she still experienced difficulties in her everyday life, such as feelings of loneliness and lack of meaningful occupation (as she had no employment). She re-established a much better relationship with her mother which helped her feel less lonely, but her learning disability meant she was still vulnerable within her community and thus continued to experience some justifiable anxiety, though at a much reduced level.

Conclusion

In this chapter I have attempted to show how fear pervades much of life for many people with learning disabilities and its long fingers are insidiously apparent in many everyday experiences. Some people have experienced fear to a far greater extent if they have been victims of such horrors as intimidation, abuse or war, as many have.

In the art therapy vignettes I illustrated the possible use of projective identification as a form of unconscious communication and splitting as a primitive form of defence. Tony slowly developed his understanding of some issues including his tolerance of frustration, and found a means to reduce agitation through image making, but was still subject to very primitive thought processes chiefly governed by bodily sensations.

Cheryl had a more developed capacity for communication and thinking but I felt she was unable to progress beyond splitting as a defence, and her behaviour was also governed by bodily sensations when she could not understand what she was experiencing. Art therapy seemed to help her to communicate more effectively with her carers, and appropriate liaison assisted the development of a better shared understanding and thus a calmer experience of home life. Laura also seemed to use splitting as a defence and found it hard to think about the experiences that made her fearful, including her own destructiveness, but was capable of moving beyond splitting towards integration of her good and bad feelings. This gave her the capacity to learn what she had previously been unable to understand, in terms of life skills, a greatly increased emotional vocabulary and an understanding of how her emotions and behaviour were linked. This development enabled her to make far-reaching changes in her life. Although Cheryl and Laura both made idealised images, for Laura this appeared to be a conscious choice. For the therapist, the splitting can be confusing, as it renders the split-off parts difficult to work with; for some people it is not possible to let go of those defences and develop more sophisticated ones, whereas others can.

The people with severe learning disabilities in the opening vignette all reacted in different ways in response to fear; had the incident not been witnessed it would have been hard for the staff to understand these reactions, as the people were unable to verbally communicate what had happened to make them so fearful. In addition, their reactions might not even have been understood to have been responses to fear, and I think this is a common situation for people whose communication is complicated by their lack of speech and resulting dependence on other means to facilitate understanding. In such circumstances a lack of understanding of the cause of the reaction can result in the wrong approach being taken by carers in response.

In this chapter I discussed the complexity of the development of thinking, communication and understanding and the consequences when that development is incomplete. I hope this discussion will have shown why so much fear and anxiety is felt by people with learning disabilities. Add to these difficulties some of the other problems people encounter, such as autism with its attendant terrors, and the frightening experience of epilepsy, and we can begin to appreciate that the fingers of fear can be much more deep-rooted and pervasive for people with learning disabilities.

The attack on the therapist's thinking is a difficult aspect of the work with people who have learning disabilities, which, if it remains unrecognised and understanding is not sought through supervision and/or peer support, is a lost source of valuable information. Likewise, unconscious processes need to be understood and brought to consciousness, particularly if the therapist is working with people who have severe learning disabilities, because the level of projective identification used as a form of communication is high, and has a considerable impact on the therapist's counter-transference. Some individuals who cannot communicate fear verbally will find other means of communicating their experience so the therapist feels the fear too, while others who engage in splitting as a defence may protect themselves and the therapist from their difficult feelings.

The fear the therapist experiences may not be restricted to unconscious processes but may also be a result of risk of actual physical injury, and appropriate risk management procedures must be part of the planning process for a therapeutic intervention with people who challenge staff in these ways. In addition, therapists need to become cognizant of underlying and unacknowledged fear within themselves and their colleagues that can be defended against by staff presenting a false impression of fearlessness.

In art therapy, fear can be acknowledged, addressed and its power reduced, when client and art therapist work together to gain a shared understanding of the difficulties the individual faces every day in communication and understanding.

References

Bion, W. [1967] (1993). *Second Thoughts*. London: H. Karnac (Books) Ltd.

De Groeff, J. (1999). 'Mental Handicaps: A Dark Continent', in J. De Groef and E. Heinemann (eds) *Psychoanalysis and Mental Handicap*, Chapter 4. London: Free Association Books.

Department of Health (1983). Mental Health Act..

Department of Health (1990).National Health Service and Community Care Act.

Foster, A. (2001). 'The Duty to Care and the Need to Split', *Journal of Social Work Practice* 15, 1: 81–90.

Gomez, L. (1997). *An Introduction to Object Relations*. London: Free Association Books.

Hallam, J. (1984). 'Regression and Ego Integration in Art Therapy with Mentally Handicapped People', in *Conference Proceedings*, Hertfordshire College of Art and Design, 29–30 November 1984, pp. 8–15.

Huet, V. (2011). 'Art Therapy-based Organisational Consultancy: A Session at Tate Britain', *International Journal of Art Therapy: Formerly Inscape* 16, 1: 3–13.

McGee, J., Menolascino, F., Hobbs, D. and Menousek, P. (1987). *Gentle Teaching:A Non-Aversive Approach to Helping Persons with Mental Retardation*. New York: Human Sciences Press.

Rees, M. (1998). 'Clinical Supervision in Art Therapy. Is it Really "Super"?', in M. Rees (ed.) *Drawing on Difference: Art Therapy with People who have Learning Difficulties.* London and New York: Routledge.

Schaverien, J. (2007) 'Framing Enchantment: Countertransference in Analytical Art Psychotherapy Supervision', in J. Schaverien and C. Case (eds) *Supervision of Art Psychotherapy. A Theoretical and Practical Handbook.* London and New York: Routledge.

Segal, H. (1988a). *Introduction to the Work of Melanie Klein*. London: H. Karnac (Books) Ltd. Reprinted in 2008.

Segal, H. (1988b). 'Notes on Symbol Formation', in E. Spillius (ed.) *Melanie Klein Today: Developments in Theory and Practice*. London and New York: Routledge.

Sinason, V. (1992). *Mental Handicap and the Human Condition*. London: Routledge.

Tipple, R. (1992). 'Art Therapy with People Who Have Severe Learning Difficulties', in D. Waller and A. Gilroy (eds) *Art Therapy: A Handbook*, Chapter 6. Buckingham and Bristol: Open University Press.

Tustin, F. (1992). *Autistic States in Children*, Revised Edition. London and New York: Routledge.

Wood, C. (1997). 'Facing Fear with People Who Have a History of Psychosis', *Inscape* 2, 2: 41–48.

Part VI

Powerlessness

Chapter 8

'It makes me jump when I fall over'

Quentin Bruckland

Introduction

In this chapter I focus on one man's severe feelings of powerlessness when living with a learning disability and refractory epilepsy. Firstly I look at what is meant by refractory epilepsy and I discuss its impact in terms of learning disabilities, its consequences and the recurrent effects of shame. Then, using case material, I explore a course of individual art therapy and how it was used to:

*   Lessen the self-defeating patterns and destructive effects of shame by developing a realistic sense of choice and a positive sense of self.
*   Encourage a realistic awareness of communication beyond the unresolved threats and frustrations that can be a consequence of living with refractory epilepsy and learning disabilities.
*   Develop a resourceful sense of self-awareness by acknowledging and coming to terms with unresolved vulnerability and sharing destructive and unspoken feelings of shame.

The clinical facts, the complex unique perceptions of persistent symptoms and their impact, psychological and social, experienced by this population (Espie and Kerr 1997; McGrother *et al.* 2006) need to be thoughtfully acknowledged before we can truly get to grips with the sense of shame and powerlessness affecting someone's sense of self-worth.

Epilepsy

Epilepsy is a severe neurological condition affecting as many as 44 per cent of people who live with a learning disability (Bowley and Kerr 2000; Morgan *et al.* 2003; Kerr *et al.* 2009). The more severe the learning disability, the greater the chance of contracting epilepsy. Refractory epilepsies are resistant to optimal seizure control by prescribed medicine. As a result an individual is left with a sense of uncertainty from the sudden recurrent seizures and a difficult collection of potentially disabling symptoms (Whitten and Griffiths 2007; Elger and Schmidt 2008).

Refractory epilepsies inflict a mixture of disabilities and harmful consequences from a complex relationship between neurological, physical, psychological and social symptoms (ibid.). These symptoms impact on wide-reaching areas of a person's life by triggering an underlying vulnerability to shame over and above the harsh reality of seizure activity (Raty *et al.* 2007, 2009).

Here is a stirring description given by a man I worked with in art therapy that illustrates brilliantly the directness and the recurring helplessness when living with epilepsy:

> Imagine turning around and you see a foot away from your face a HGV travelling at great speed. You know it's going to hit you instantly and there is nothing you can do to stop it hitting you. That's the only way I can describe my fear before going into a seizure.

A high-recurring seizure frequency combined with underlying intellectual deficits can leave an individual with uncertainty, emotional disruption and negative self-belief regarding future situations. This can trigger problems with control, well-being and the management of the condition itself (Ring *et al.* 2007, 2009; Elger and Schmidt 2008). This can prompt anxiety and depression and erode a person's confidence on a daily basis (Ring *et al.* 2007; Whitten and Griffiths 2007). The frequent and disruptive nature of seizures has a profound influence on choices made about life activities, control of basic functions and/or quality of independent personal care (Ring *et al.* 2007, 2009).

Epilepsies can encourage and maintain feelings of helplessness to a destructive degree for those vulnerable in this population (Tedman 1995). This can devastate any sense of self and add further pressure on an already vulnerable capacity for coping with daily functional skills. The lack of self-reliability and the consistent disruption in daily life can cause a shameful fear of failure (Ring *et al.* 2009). This has the potential to overstretch any existing reserve or coping resource increasing burdened feelings of inadequacy due to amplified dependency and reduced capacity to make appropriate choices with capable decisions. The diminished functional skills can be a direct consequence of epileptic brain activity (seizures) especially in the case of early childhood diagnosis of epilepsy (Sillanpaa 2004; Ring *et al.* 2007, 2009) and can influence a confident, able capacity for making informed, suitably valued and independent decisions. This in turn can pervasively affect any quality of life and self-belief through a lack of both real and perceived belief in self-control.

Living with epilepsy from early childhood leaves someone without any long-term insight and experience of good health, making this population feel severely disabled, over-protected and shamefully dependent into adulthood. Real or perceived, the outlook of never fully recovering can further enforce harmful and negative effects on an already low self-confidence. Living with seizures that lead to shameful experiences can cause intense hopeless despair if these harsh realities are openly recognised in public. The exposure of this shamed part of oneself can be difficult to acknowledge or come to terms with and so is often hidden due to a fear of feeling stigmatised as epileptic (Raty *et al.* 2009).

Learning disability

Living with a learning disability can often increase one's basic vulnerability when trying to convey complex emotional information or when making choices concerning one's needs and well-being (Manners and Russ 2006b; Kerr *et al.* 2009). Living with a realistic awareness of your own inability to grasp or control the direct outcome of a situation and the effect on your own communication aspirations is difficult for any person to cope with on a daily basis. Living with a constraint on choice or consensual opportunities has the potential to reduce satisfying experiences, increase distress and cause behavioural problems and feelings of inadequacy (Ring *et al.* 2009). As a result of the reduction of consensual prospects a person may feel they have a difficulty in making choices, or they may make poor choices from the restricted options available. This can then negatively affect their own sense of self-value with control and self-motivation, and after discovery reinforce a deep sense of shame (Price 2002; Manners and Carruthers 2006a).

Living with a cognitive impairment, continuous complex emotional needs and recurrent unmet needs can feel overpowering and self-affecting (Harris 1993; Kay 2003;). The unmet need to express and untangle these difficulties can often increase a sense of inadequacy, negative apprehension and feelings of frustrating helplessness (Scheepers *et al.* 2004; Ring *et al.* 2007, 2009; Whitten and Griffiths 2007). These negative feelings are often added to by association with any previous failed attempts to communicate, express or name needs and desires – the person is simply unable to describe the patterns in life they experience.

Historically, many services have not met needs realistically or been supportive of the aspirations of people with learning disabilities (Kay 2003). Whether real or perceived, the fear of failure denies a person both feelings of control as well as the benefit of having the time and the quality of choice in the pace of our world today. Fears of shame can be helplessly difficult for the individual by remaining undisclosed, hidden or unmet and can generate a general self-perception of being insignificant and frustratingly helpless. People living with learning disabilities need to be able to use language that is appropriate to them personally and have choice in how and with whom they communicate in the outside world. They may need to be supported in identifying and utilising appropriate communication tools, be they words, pictures, actions or bodily movements. They will often need to be given time to understand the effects of their own specific decision-making processes. The support provided should allow the person to have a realistic understanding of their own experiences and choices allowing them to gain a sense of control without wanting to hide, avoid or just dispose of difficult feelings.

The very existence of new and different choices can generate feelings of inadequacy, especially when living with a compromised ability to negotiate life in what may sometimes feel like an over-protected and complicated outside world for some people with learning disabilities. Difficulties with finding the right words to accurately communicate and understand their own new choices in a new and different situation can lead to frustration. This can have a confusing 'knock-on' effect by inducing feelings of helpless self-belief, avoidance and/or self-isolating behaviour if it's not dealt with and resolved (Ring *et al.* 2007, 2009; Elger and Schmidt 2008).

Powerlessness and shame

The need to feel in control of one's life, mind and bodily functions on a daily basis is a basic human characteristic. Making authentic choices empowers a person to experience a sense of control and can provide a way of restoring a sense of power to a previously powerless state (Lansky 2005; Rustomjee 2009). A person self-functions by ongoing development through a continuous influence and interaction with their past and present experiences. These life events and experiences can connect the person to the outside world and this then becomes their own world of experience.

Powerlessness is a psychological state that can reawaken internalised and ingrained negative overwhelming experiences (Cook 1994; Lansky 2005). These can cause and maintain a deep vulnerability to feeling the shame that is associated with a previous experience (Sullivan 1996). Living with a severe long-term condition can threaten a person's core sense of self-image and self-value triggering a whole range of negative feelings (Kirby 1988; Raty *et al.* 2009). If these experiences involve a recurrent, sudden, confusing change of an unavoidable nature, they will ultimately lead to a conscious awareness of these shameful experiences frequently recurring (Kirby 1988; Kaufman 1996; Lansky 2005), especially when there is a complete loss of control, anticipation and choice associated with the experience. If not resolved, there is the increased risk of these feelings frequently resurfacing in the future and the experiences having a dehumanising effect on the person. If left to manifest, this can cause an unbearable disruption with the potential to erode or significantly destroy a person's ability to maintain important relationship bonds and so cause social avoidance.

However, it is important to be aware that when a person shares the unresolved experience this can cause a further sense of vulnerability following a humiliating exposure of a concealed problem and having to come to terms with the person's own deflated idea of who they are. The key emotional role of a shaming experience is its negative impact on a person's core sense of self and identity leading to a conscious exposure or awareness of inadequate fear of failure. A conscious awareness of shame can often be felt when a person is exposed to an emotional state of acknowledging oneself as overwhelmingly inadequate, vulnerable and intensely different in the presence of others. These feelings cause intense humiliation creating a negative effect on the person's self-esteem which involves the shaping and influencing of the person's sense of self (Lansky 2005).

Hidden shame is often severe and operates out of view, involving a need to defend, hide or ignore intense self-defeating patterns and feelings that negatively affect self-worth and self-respect. Unpleasant experiences may be suppressed, bypassed or concealed by a need to prevent and shield against any conscious awareness of having a flaw of this nature. This is often due to the fact that pre-verbal experiences of feeling powerless are very challenging and difficult to articulate particularly where there is the frustrating absence of any adult language to make sense of such feelings (Sullivan 1996; Lansky 2005). These experiences may be associated with feelings of failure from unresolved or unmet needs and a lack of ability to provide a sense of control. This is often presented in a physical somatic way, defending against a need to disown and dispose of the ill or bad part of the self.

Behaviour such as rage and aggression are often externalised reactions to blame associated with upset, unsupported or unmet needs that can create feelings of being socially shamed and helpless (Lansky 2005). A healthy self originates from the experiences of important others meeting a person's particular needs and any different experience can potentially trigger an active sense of rejection and shame.

Introduction to Thomas

What follows is a unique personal journey of a man called Thomas. He is in his thirties and has lived with a learning disability and refractory epilepsies from early childhood. He was referred to art therapy because he was becoming severely withdrawn and uncommunicative and had presented some reactive aggressive outbursts during the daytime. Any encouragement to do anything other than isolate himself in his room would exacerbate these behaviours. His attendance at any activities was sporadic and as a result he lacked any purposeful interactions outside his home.

On interviewing Thomas I came across a shy man presenting severe low self-esteem who appeared to be withdrawn, deflated and vulnerable. I felt I needed to offer this man a sensitive experience that was realistic and flexible but consistent. I was very conscious of not wanting to impose or rob him of his own language, actions or active expression and how he approached making art in the session. I felt a strong need to display to him a realistic belief in his capabilities so that he could develop a sense of control and experience a real sense of supported choice. I did not wish to add to his sense of feeling inadequate in life, but I did want to encourage a realistic outlook by visually retaining the significance of his experiences to capture his own self-appraisal that had upset his own command of self-belief.

I felt the sessions would help provide Thomas the opportunity to identify hidden problems and return to these by communicating and identifying choices with the aim of improving self-esteem, motivation and a purposeful sense of self. I was aware when taking this referral that it was highly unrealistic to expect an absolute alleviation of all the frustrations that Thomas had. I felt that by seeing Thomas' own account of his situation, we could identify his authentic yet concealed perspective and lost voice. We could then enable a visual and verbal bridging of the gaps in his abilities and assist in some simple, realistic and achievable under-standing of his own perception of fears, destructive obstacles and their fearful effects. Hopefully, Thomas would then be able to deal with the daily insults on the sense of self more effectively. Ongoing communication between sessions helped in motivating an acknowledgement of control by encouraging a sense of meaningful purpose and value in his need for an improved sense of self. By adding an achievable and realistic sense of control as a point of reference we could start to meet and challenge Thomas' basic lack of self-consistency and the imposed effects of these profound feelings.

The art therapy sessions

Our first session was on a spring morning. Thomas arrived on time with his coat fastened, buttoned and zipped tightly up to his chin. With a smile, he refused to take off his coat. He initially said very little and kept checking the buttons and zip to see if they were still buttoned and zipped up. His coat was pulled up covering some part of his face, an air of self-critical inadequacy or inferiority surrounding him. Being concealed appeared to be the known place for him – a normal daily hiding place. His physical presence and response to most situations or questions seemed to be one of being on the periphery, hidden and with a desire to be invisible to other people. His coat and body language implied an obvious impenetrable defensive and protective layer around him. He had a slight lean to his stance. Thomas was completely sealed up where nothing got out, nothing could get at him and no one would see past the obvious coated artificial protection holding him tightly together.

He would arrive at the art room quietly with an intense look in his eye and his coat fastened right up to his neck. He appeared defensive as if he didn't want to be seen in the session or by the outside world.

Thomas' first piece of art was of a striking graphic image of a baby's pram floating with nothing around it but his name and age on the top and bottom of the paper (Plate 8.1). The image was created over a period of seven sessions. He often presented what I thought to be a symbolic abstract connection to the art that he made. Together, we explored possible feelings about being with other people and about whether or not he could trust them. Thomas' main communication sparked by this image seemed to be focused on how he felt about his life; separate, unseen, unheard and helplessly dependent. I was particularly struck by the fact that there was no person visible or even hiding in his image. I wondered about the possibility of Thomas feeling directly and indirectly devalued by others who may have good and bad intentions. We also spoke about how he might be perceived by others who did not truly understand his support needs as a man. We explored some of his life experiences and how these had left him with a recurring feeling of being unable to do anything in what felt like a life of complications and feelings relating to refusal or 'no's' on a daily basis. Thomas often simply shrugged his shoulders, looking resigned and confused. So much of his life was not being seen or was being shamefully submerged, made invisible, unnamed and unknown under a shield of dependency. His movements when talking about this image were a dramatic visual introduction to his own perception of the absence of any independent lifestyle.

Both Thomas and his image seemed to magnify his sense of remote isolation and, I felt, communicated the humiliating aspects of his life that felt highly inappropriate for his age. He told me that this was a picture of how life makes him feel. He said 'I live in a funny upside-down world' and talked of a need to feel supported, looked after and loved due to the nature of the frequent uncertain, intrusive and fragile states from seizures. He also expressed a desire to hide from all the uncomfortable feelings associated with this.

I became aware of a sense of Thomas being all wrapped up with the medical management of his condition and what was professionally or medically most appropriate for him. This seemed to have indirectly generated feelings of helplessness and of being left with no true identity or sense of who he was as a person. The shrugging of his shoulders became a common sign of him feeling and showing helpless shame in the session. He would often say 'weak' as a way to describe how he related to the imagery and his feelings of inadequacy. In all his images his name and age often appear in bold writing. This seemed to be Thomas' wish to be taken into full account: 'me and my age'. There was a sense of a battle that he felt was beyond his own personal control regardless of his age. I felt that he was effectively communicating and depicting that he was powerless to stop his current pattern of ill-health.

Thomas would arrive in the session and quickly become deeply absorbed in what appeared to be a practical, eager aspiration to create art. He worked in an intensely focused manner, slowly experimenting and getting in touch with a kind of needed contemplative meaning and choice. He worked very close to his image, never initiating conversation with me but putting his own unique visual vocabulary and dialogue on paper. Thomas would answer questions without moving either his hands or eyes away from his art making. He worked from the moment he arrived until the session ended. He placed the pens neatly to one side in a very polite, private, ordered and contemplative manner.

During our eighth session a rattle slowly appeared from a dot-to-dot construction (see Figure 8.1). The image gradually came into view as Thomas worked in complete silence. It seemed to me as though he wanted me to see, feel and experience *waiting* whilst he slowly put his creation together. He would often laugh and look out of the corner of his eye at me. After he had finished his image, we talked about the connection between the pram and his independence and what the rattle symbolised. I felt that the making of this image illustrated something about his frustration of dependency – having to wait due to ill-health, stay safely in one place to recover – and how these experiences had triggered early childlike feelings. These images allowed us to view both hidden and obvious feelings of frustration. In the weeks that followed he calmly made artwork that realistically and accurately reflected his situation, which we explored together.

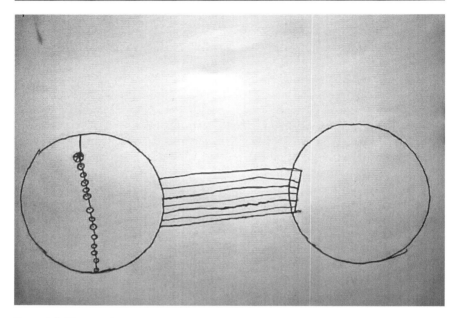

Figure 8.1 Thomas: Rattle.

The calm, concise conversations we had at this stage of the therapy centred on his self-image as a result of negative experiences and their incredibly sensitive effects. Thomas made it very clear that how he perceived himself was strongly influenced by how he felt others saw and valued him and that this was often connected to a disliked self-image that he had of himself. The artwork presented us both with a visual association to his life and boosted communication by sharing these links. We talked about the importance of feeling valued and the difficulties involved when looking at ourselves as unimportant, insignificant, despised and powerless.

This provided Thomas with an approach to convey his responses to difficulties, start to deal with experiences and to deal with what it felt like to live with recurrent negative feelings of inability in his life. I felt that the image and the session allowed for some deeper understanding of emotions where a trust of his own feelings could create opportunities for him to be properly present with me and promised an expansion of a healthier well-being and sense of self.

His 'coated' approach to the sessions started to lessen. We discussed the change and the reason why he did not keep the coat on during the session now. He said that he felt he wanted to be more part of things here in the session and taking his coat off meant to him that he could do more of this and be comfortable. He said the coat was in the way of his drawing and was feeling like the problem he had with uncomfortable feelings. Thomas went on to say that he never stayed too long in one place with other people so why take off your coat anyway. This was an opening in the session where we could discuss his avoidance of other people, situations and the reason Thomas isolates himself. He spoke of feelings of failure and inadequacy from his own awareness of the effects on his perception of his fragile ability to interact, communicate and feel comfortable to be able to be included anywhere. We discussed the protective purpose of the coat, an object for holding himself together by cocooning himself. In using this approach he felt he could contain and defend himself from perceived feelings of rejection, feeling indifferent, out of control and unlovable. We were both comfortable using this simple but effective approach to highlight insightful and dynamic benefits that have various meanings to convey hidden feelings and effects on his life.

Thomas' need to keep his coat on lessened further and ended when his need to hide was replaced by his own natural and appropriate skill to creatively communicate these profound and complex feelings of powerlessness. Once these experiences and influences were out in view for us to name, know and think about he started to make connections to these negative effects and in doing so made them less fearful and a more tolerable influence on a wide variety of environments. A large part of the therapy was made in the capacity of us seeing, recognising, communicating and making appropriate meanings to and from the art that he was making. This was especially true when deciphering his perceptions, beliefs about his feelings of being powerless and making simple adaptive connections with his art and myself. New observed meanings fused with the artwork serving previously unmet, undiscovered and different experiences of explaining the effects of being powerless and shamed. I found that allowing him the value of choice and the importance of the experience of being trusted with information gave him a taste of self-control and self-value easing his initial sense of feeling powerless.

After making the image of the rattle Thomas made some images directed at his masculinity, focusing around his core needs, feelings and desires possibly showing how he felt powerless in the face of being misunderstood. Feeling out of control, indifferent, experiencing direct and indirect rejection and having feelings of being unloved seemed to be due to living with unresolved shame. Words alone would not have been adequate for the complexity of these blended feelings as they were hard to make any sense of. We experienced together the waiting to share and in his own time to express and understand his unique communication. There were moments within Thomas' therapy process when I felt deeply isolated with a sense of being helpless and of time floating by in an intrusive manner too complex to comprehend and understand.

One of these later images seemed to really express the diversity of his feelings and the different strands of symptoms involved in feeling powerless. Colour blocks spanned the entire page; waving across the page like a feeling of intense frustration all contained on one page. During the making of this complex image there was complete silence. I stayed with the defining quiet and the image slowly developed. His relationship to this image was complex, mirrored by the intense suspense, silence, sense of uncertainty and potential unknown nature of it. The art conveyed and served a significant purpose in making some meaning and easing uncertainty.

The art slowly made bearable the intensity of these feelings. After he created the image he communicated by laughing out loud, looked at the lines of colour then slowly folded the paper in two and quickly ripped the paper to pieces. He slowly collected up all the pieces and neatly put them in the bin. The loud ripping sound tore through the session after such a quiet, intense, complex contemplation of not knowing and waiting. This was a little startling. He noticed and laughed quietly saying, 'It makes me jump when I fall over.'

This was a powerful point in our work together where he allowed himself to be vulnerable and exposed and to trust his worth of himself and the session. The importance of this experience for both of us was trust. There was a direct need from Thomas to have an acknowledgment of this sudden and instant event. How intense the quiet was beforehand, the slow calm folding of the paper and then the sudden loud tear through the session. This seemed to be an enactment of a seizure mimicking the uncertainty, intense and intrusive feelings before a seizure and the ensuing devastating sense of being powerless due to the often-unstoppable episode (seizure). We talked about this being a kind of playful shock within our session but also acknowledged the uncertain, fearful, anxious and inescapable distress that can follow a seizure. We also discussed the significant feeling of being powerless due to the long silence, the sudden laughter, the crashing and the ripping sound entering the session. His disposal of the paper was a lengthy process. The picking up of the pieces was as important as the actual image making. 'The need to pick up after a scattering', he said while collecting the pieces, 'You can pick yourself up, all of yourself and carry on, get up and on.' A simple effective sense of relief and pride came over Thomas' face from the explosive act he had produced and experienced. Through a lengthy discussion we both witnessed acceptance and awareness of his perceptions of himself and he shared his uncertainty of feeling powerless during events with me. Naming his recurrent, immediate, hidden, private feelings and perceptions allowed us to view the harmful sense of being powerless and its effects, his reasons good or bad for the self-isolation. This provided us with the understanding of some potential for simple enabling approaches to experience choice.

This was a different encounter to what he had previously experienced as hidden, solitary and isolated contemplation. Working on holding onto thoughts and holding onto very profound and real feelings was frightening, but this work brought about a new chance to evoke a different outcome of control in the session for Thomas. This enactment was diverse, angrily dramatic, complex, moving, frustrating, confusing but above all humbling. Thomas said, 'I have shown you my embarrassment.' Sharing this enactment with me illustrated his own powerful and very real emotions performed by his own creative thinking and a desire to communicate with me. It seemed important that I was there to witness and acknowledge his enactment. We both experienced his own description of his sense of being powerless and his ongoing loss of control. There was no way this could be hidden, not experienced and so not thought about. The sharing, the trust and being able to find a sense of meaning within his creativity was, for Thomas, a massive lessening of his sense of powerlessness and negative sense of self. His own experience of my reaction seemed to lessen his shame. There was something very enabling about this experience for Thomas, far away from his shared experiences of feeling shamed. One of the most touching aspects of this work was that Thomas could be present without his coat on. He allowed me to see him without feeling shamed. This was a vital emphasis of his capacity to experience something other than to feel disadvantaged, powerless and shamed. He found this through a sense of trust and potency in the creative relationship by simply communicating meaningful insights of his sense of value and naming these important meanings. These experiences made sense of who he is apart from just being recurrently out of control and unwell.

Thomas' awareness or perception of control had manifested itself in intense frustration and uncertainty. This in turn supported an unstable sense of self and a loss of control of body image in what felt like a never-ending cycle of vulnerability and an ensuing incapable state. The consequence was significant withdrawal and negative mood responses producing a pervasive inadequate and negative self-perception of control, burden and shame. Being able to communicate, name, describe and hold onto the image for the next week and from the previous sessions allowed Thomas and me some connection in the session. Rather than being cut off from communication due to his isolated helpless state there was a subtle but vital step in feeling and in having some potential in life. It was strikingly powerful for me to witness, and very liberating for him to share in the presence of someone else.

Relying on words alone would have been inappropriate and would have impeded any clear description for Thomas to put together this profoundly, and at times devastatingly, complicated puzzle of thoughts. This would be especially true if you take his memory disturbances into account that leave him with an array of processing problems due to living with recurrent attacks, absences, loss of time and basic information. These significantly affected his abilities when remembering daily events. This left him with feelings of inadequacy and negative preconceptions of his basic ability to interact, communicate and be included in any daily existence. Thomas found some motivation to embrace the session, the art and me as his therapist. By doing so, he connected to his difficult feelings and was able to make some realistic sense out of his own fear of being helpless that had engulfed him with a further withdrawn secondary disability.

Conclusion

The relationship between the art, the studio and our therapeutic alliance provided an environment in which Thomas felt motivated. He increased his own capacity to communicate about the negative impact of his epilepsy. I felt that his emotional perception was helped through using images, physical movement and words. This allowed Thomas to have a realistic and appropriate sense of control to confront, oppose and lessen his magnified sense of powerlessness and shame by reflecting upon the images made.

Thomas communicated in the session by choosing a language that relied on the useful information relevant to both his core feeling and his own capacity to comprehend these difficult effects. This on its own provided a sense of self-control, motivating a simple enabling approach where decision making and/or wanting to be heard could be triggered. I felt that helped to reduce Thomas' need to withdraw, self-isolate and be uncommunicative and instead enhanced his sense of well-being and self-worth. His expansive adaptive connections with his art and with me allowed him to be seen and to communicate hidden and unresolved effects. Thomas' passive, hidden and, at times, aggressive experience was lessened by using a more appropriate language for his own specific capacity. This helped Thomas to make sense of intrusively profound troubling effects, events and experiences and also allowed him to see himself as more than a powerless, shamed person who wanted to withdraw and hide.

References

Bowley, C. and Kerr, M. (2000). 'Epilepsy and Intellectual Disability', *Journal of Intellectual Disability Research* 44: 529–543.

Cook, D. R. (1994). *Internalised Shame Scale: Professional Manual*. Menomonie, Wisconsin: Channel Press.

Elger, C. E. and Schmidt, D. (2008). 'Modern Management of Epilepsy: A Practical Approach', *Epilepsy & Behaviour* 12: 501–539.

Espie, C. A. and Kerr, M. (1997). 'Learning Disability and Epilepsy: A Review of Available Outcome Measures and Position Statement on Development Priorities', *Seizure* 6: 337–350.

Harris, P. (1993). 'The Nature of Aggressive Behaviour Amongst People with Learning Disabilities (Mental Handicap) in a Single Health District', *Journal of Intellectual Disabilities Research* 37, 3: 221–242.

Kaufman, G. (1996). *The Psychology of Shame: Theory and Treatment of Shame-Based Syndromes*, Second Edition. New York: Springer.

Kay, B. (2003). 'Changing Philosophy in Learning Disability', in A. Markwick and A. Parish (eds) *Learning Disabilities: Themes and Perspectives*. Edinburgh: Butterworth-Heinemann.

Kerr, M., Turky, A. and Huber, B. (2009). 'The Psychological Impact of Epilepsy in Adults with an Intellectual Disability', *Epilepsy & Behaviour* 15, 2: S26–S30.

Kirby, D. (1988). 'Shame and the Use of Health Care Services', *Inscape*, Spring: 11–13.

Lansky, M. R. (2001). 'Hidden Shame, Working Through, and the Problem of Forgiveness in the Tempest', *Journal of the American Psychoanalytic Association* 49: 1005–1033.

Lansky, M. R. (2005). 'Hidden Shame', *Journal of the American Psychoanalytic Association* 53: 865–890.

Manners, P. J. and Carruthers, E. (2006a). 'Living with Learning Difficulties: Emma's Story', *British Journal of Learning Difficulties* 34, 4: 206–210.

Manners, P. J. and Russ, M. (2006b). 'Working Reflexively in Learning Difficulties: What Emma Taught Us', *British Journal of Learning Disabilities* 34, 4: 211–214.

McGrother, C., Bhaumik, S. and Thorp, C. (2006) 'Epilepsy in Adults with Intellectual Disabilities: Prevalence, Associations and Service Implications', *Seizure* 15: 376–386.

Morgan, C. L., Baxter, H. and Kerr, M. P. (2003) 'Prevalence of Epilepsy and Associated Health Service Utilization and Morality Among Patients with Intellectual Disabilities', *American Journal of Mental Retardation* 108, 5: 293–300.

Price, L. A. (2002). 'The Connections Among Psychosocial Issues, Adult Development and Self-Determination', in L. C. Brinkerhoff, J. M. McGuire and S. F. Shaw (eds) *Postsecondary Education and Transition for Students with Learning Difficulties*. Austin, TX: PRO-ED.

Raty, L. K. A., Larsson, G., Starrin, B., Bodil, M. and Larsson, W. (2009). 'Epilepsy Patients' Conception of Epilepsy as a Phenomenon', *Journal of Neuroscience Nursing* 41, 4: 201–210.

Raty, L. K. A., Soderfelt, B. A. and Wilde Larson, B. M. (2007). 'Daily Life in Epilepsy: Patients' Experiences Described by Emotions', *Epilepsy & Behaviour* 10: 389–396.

Ring, H., Zia, A., Linderman, S. and Himlok, K. (2007). 'Interactions Between Seizure Frequency, Psychopathology, and Severity of Intellectual Disability in a Population with Epilepsy and a Learning Disability', *Epilepsy & Behaviour* 11: 92–97.

Ring, H., Zia, A., Bateman, N., Williams, E., Lindeman, S. and Himlok, K. (2009). 'How is Epilepsy Treated in People with a Learning Disability? A Retrospective Observational Study of 183 Individuals', *Seizure* 18: 264–268.

Rustomjee, S. (2009). 'The Solitude and Agony of Unbearable Shame', *Group Analysis* 42: 143.

Scheepers, B., Salahudeen, S. and Morelli, J. (2004). 'Two-year Outcome Audit in an Adult Learning Disability Population with Refractory Epilepsy', *Seizure* 13: 529–533.

Sillanpaa, M. (2004). 'Learning Disability: Occurrence and Long-term Consequences in Childhood-onset Epilepsy', *Epilepsy & Behaviour* 5: 937–944.

Sullivan, H. S. (1996). 'Internalisation of Shame', in G. Kaufman (ed.) *The Psychology of Shame: Theory and Treatment of Shame-Based Syndromes*, Second Edition. New York: Springer.

Tedman, S. (1995). 'Development of a Scale to Measure Core Beliefs and Perceived Self-efficacy in Adults with Epilepsy', *Seizure* 4: 221–231.

Whitten, E. and Griffiths, A. (2007). 'Implementing Epilepsy Guidelines within a Learning Disability Service', *Seizure* 16: 471–478.

Part VII

Self and identity

Chapter 9

'The Beast can scream'

Stephanie Bull

Introduction

Research shows that if a person is given the label of having learning disabilities or intellectual disabilities this will usually dominate and suppress all other aspects of their identity such as gender, ethnic origin, religion and sexuality; it becomes their primary identity and has a permanence that is difficult to escape (Beart *et al.* 2005).

In this final case example, I explore the theme of self and identity with some help from a man called David B (pseudonym). The perceived burden of having a diagnosis of Down's syndrome and the day-to-day impact this had on David B's relationships and his sense of self and identity were at the core of our work together. He battled against having an identity that had been imposed upon him by society's tendency to want to stereotype. David B managed to break away from this and now chooses to present himself first and foremost as a gay man.

Here, I consider David B's art therapy journey as a process of self-discovery and we focus on three pieces of artwork that he made at significant points along the way. Within this chapter, he shares with you his personal thoughts about his life and his artwork. David B's own words are shown in italics.

All names of people and venues, other than my own, are pseudonyms that David B has chosen.

Clinical context

I worked as part of a multidisciplinary community learning disability team. David B was referred to the team because the staff supporting him on a day-to-day basis were struggling to manage some very challenging behaviours such as arson and over-sexualised interactions with others. He was initially assessed by a nurse and was then referred on to me for art therapy as it was felt that he would benefit from the opportunity to explore his emotional state within the safe framework that I could offer.

When I first met David B, just to introduce myself and explain to him how art therapy might work, I was immediately struck by how articulate he was and I was also amused by his sense of humour. As our work developed, he was constantly surprising me and pulling me beyond the limitations of the learning disability label. He was enthusiastic about beginning art therapy and I felt from the outset that the potential was there for some powerful work. We agreed that individual work would be more beneficial than group work and we also acknowledged that he would need to be supported by a member of staff from his home to travel to and from our sessions. This meant that I often saw the member of staff briefly in the waiting area before and/or after every session.

While initially we arranged for six 50-minute assessment sessions, it soon became clear this would need to be a long and intensive piece of work; in fact, our work together continued for nearly two years.

Introducing David B

A short piece about my life

(Written by David B with some support from Bev, the manager of his care home.)

In my family there is my mum, Deirdre, and then of course me. I have two brothers, Steven and Stuart, my godfather, Brian, and Gran, who is the only grandparent I have that is still alive. I have my dad, Justin, and loads of cousins, a few in London and two in Sussex. I used to have a dog but that was given to a builder when I was young. Then years later, Carla moved into the family home and brought her pet parrot with her but unfortunately that died. Now I have two cats.

When I was very little, I went to nursery school and then went to primary school. Then I moved and went to senior school. I stayed there until I was a teenager and then moved as it was time for me to move on as I was getting older. I had a really good friend called Sophie and I also had a really good friend called Ted who was at the same primary and senior school as me. I really liked school and wish I was still there sometimes.

After that I went to college and learnt about gardening and farming. I enjoyed college.

At 19, I decided to move out of my family home and went to live at Southport Road and I stayed there until I was 24. On the day I moved out of Southport Road I felt nervous, I enjoyed my time at Southport Road but I felt I had to leave so I could move on. So, on 30th September, I moved out of Southport Road and into London Street. I was really looking forward to the move and was very excited.

So here I am living at London Street, enjoying life, playing football four times a week and also football tournaments. I like to do the shift input with the manager on a Friday morning and get up early to do this. I like to go down to the local pub for a pint or a glass of wine and socialise with the other people who live at the house. My first Christmas at the house I got a little nervous about going home to my family as I had not moved in very long and did not want to leave my new room but in the end I did decide I would have Christmas with my family.

I would also like to say that I am gay and enjoy my life at London Street and will be going to Gay Pride with a member of staff.

Self

Most people have a sense of something unique to them that is the essence of their individual being. This is often referred to as the *self* and the words *myself, himself, herself, yourself* and *oneself* are frequently woven into day-to-day communication. Many of us slip into the convenient illusion of thinking about the self as something that is static and singular. However, the self is never completely formed and needs to be in constant flux with many fragments that develop throughout one's lifetime.

Jung stated, 'The self is not only the centre but also the whole circumference which embraces both conscious and unconscious' (Jung 1955: paragraph 44). He acknowledged the self as something all-encompassing with aspects such as the ego and the persona being constituent parts of the whole. Where many parts exist there is also potential for conflict; as individuals we seek resolution to internal conflict and contradiction. Jung used the term *individuation* to describe a process of self-realisation and suggested that this could lead to 'an integration or completeness of the individual, who in this way approaches wholeness but not perfection' (Jung 1963: paragraph 616). Jung also recognised that it is the complex journey towards this state that is essential (Hochheimer 1969). Ideally, one eventually develops the ability to hold these internal opposites in a healthy tension and to reach what Jung referred to as the 'transcendence of all opposites'.

For many, the process of *individuation* begins with a wound to the personality, and the subsequent suffering this brings (Von Franz 1978:169). David B began his work with me at a particularly difficult time in his life. His parents had divorced a few years earlier which had caused him a great deal of pain and confusion. He had also moved out of the family home and begun sharing a supported house with four other men with learning disabilities. This had not been an easy transition and David B's behaviour became a challenge to those supporting him. I felt that beginning art therapy seemed to initiate a process of self-development and enabled David B to explore the conflict within him and ultimately reach a greater sense of wholeness.

'I feel like I want to scream'

David B seemed to need to use our first few sessions as a form of catharsis. He poured bottles of paint directly onto large pieces of paper; the paint would run and spill off the edge of the paper and then off the table and onto the floor. It often seemed to be completely out of control. I usually think of myself as being quite 'at home' with mess within the art therapy room and yet I found myself running around trying to contain the paint. I would often have piles of paper towels in each hand and I was aware of a degree of anxiety that I didn't usually experience. In this way, I was becoming increasingly involved in David B's enactment and it was clear that my role was to provide containment for his anxieties where the image alone could not.

Figure 9.1   David B: 'I feel like I want to scream'.

When David B finished a piece of work he always asked me to add a written statement to explain the painting. Figure 9.1 is an example of one of these early paintings; the statement he asked me to write was 'I feel like I want to scream.' Other paintings were given statements which included such things as 'When I feel angry I go completely silent', 'I feel really anxious' and 'David B is really stressed out inside.'

I felt these statements were his way of reflecting internal aspects back to himself and also his way of finishing each piece. This provided a sense of further containment for what otherwise felt extremely uncontained at the time.

Here is what David B says about this piece.

This one here is to get rid of all the anxieties I had un underneath . . .. um as I was doing it I was noticed I'm getting . . . rid of lot of stress . . . lot of pain and stuff like that so . . . doing it, I realised . . . getting all the tension out and writing down 'I feel like I want to scream' . . . reason why that's there . . . so I look at that and I realised . . . okay . . . whatever is making me feel down . . . will have to come out with using black paint. If I pour it out instead of painting it, it just gets rid of all the tension that I had anyway because I knew deep down I really needed to get rid of it. By looking at it now, it just reminds me of all the tension, all the anger and all the hate is out . . .

The black paint is expressing how I felt before I started doing the art therapy. When I left the session and after it was all out, I felt relieved and relaxed so . . . so now I can think . . . okay . . . it's all out . . . with black paint . . . okay . . . fantastic . . . now it's time to move on.

The Theatre

After many weeks of working in this way, David B began to seek some focus on what he was feeling inside. He switched to using materials that he could be much more in control of, including felt-tipped pens and crayons. He began to write a dialogue between two or more characters and these evolved into 'play scripts'. He would assign parts to both of us and the sessions became a mixture of him writing and then us both playing the different characters and reading out what he had written.

To develop this further we worked together to create a theatre and some puppets (see Plate 9.1) so that his scripts could really begin to come to life. His scripts worked around the same four characters, Good Bit, Bad Bit, The Queen and The Guard. The main plot revolved around finding a way to capture and contain Bad Bit. Eventually David B added some 'bars' to the front of the model and thus the theatre became a prison where Bad Bit was incarcerated.

This is what David B thought about working in this way.

Making the theatre made me realise . . . um . . . part of me wants to express it and the other part is saying okay . . . . I'm going to keep these deeper feelings down. All I've got to do is build a theatre and we'll have Good Bit and Bad Bit and The Queen and The Guard. The best bit for me was getting that out in the open by acting out these feelings I had deep down. Bad Bit expresses me realising okay there's something wrong . . . meanwhile to the Good Bit . . . The Good Bit was making me realise . . . okay I want to move on in life and I want to do good things in life. The Guard was thinking to lock the Bad Bit up in prison that's because the Bad Bit was making me do stupid things . . . and suicide attempts . . . so the Bad Bit would be locked up . . . making me realise . . . okay I want to move on and the guard decided okay I'll lock the Bad Bit up and I can carry on with what I've got in life. And um . . . the Bad Bit was making sure that I get in trouble and the Bad Bit was making sure that I get arrested by the police. So I didn't want to get arrested by the police . . . that's where the Good Bit comes in and says 'Right this is not on and it's time to move on' . . . and the Bad Bit says 'No' . . . now reason why it was in prison cos the Bad Bit was, you know, out of control, making my life miserable, making me feel low. I decided if you put the Bad Bit in prison, I can carry on with my own little life . . . instead of causing trouble and mayhem.

Identity

The term identity has been defined in various ways over the years. For some, the emphasis will be on social roles such as parent, doctor or teacher, while for others, identity is defined by personal characteristics including internal qualities and external appearance. It is also argued that one's identity always develops from social interaction and therefore that all identity is social (Beart *et al.* 2005).

How we present ourselves to others, the impression we make and how others perceive us are all part of our sense of identity. This is different to our sense of self. Jung suggests that the *persona* plays an important role in maintaining psychic health as the persona (derived from the Latin word for mask) enables us to present an illusion of ourselves to others. The self needs the persona for survival in social situations.

It is important to recognise that the development of the persona is not the same as the process of individuation. There is a danger that, for some, the persona becomes so removed from the self that even the person themself is misled by it and believes it to be their true self (Hochheimer 1969).

People with learning disabilities often find they are perceived as being part of a collective persona which has been imposed upon them. This makes it extremely difficult for each person to be received by others as an individual with their own separate identity. David B was very passionate about getting people to see beyond his Down's syndrome and accept him as a gay man.

About midway into our therapy process, David B began to access a service for young people who were exploring their sexuality. This organisation was not part of learning disability services which in itself seemed to be very important for David B as it was an opportunity for him and those supporting him to focus on other aspects of his identity.

The support he received from the staff there proved to be invaluable as he tried to shift the perception that others had of him. He expressed a wish to be part of the 'gay scene' within the city and, with the right level of support and supervision, David B was eventually able to realise this wish.

Down's syndrome

Down's syndrome (or Trisomy 21) is a chromosomal disorder and occurs when a fertilised egg contains a third chromosome 21 when normally there would be a pair. The impact this additional chromosome can have on the physical development of the person is colossal and medical conditions such as heart defects and thyroid dysfunction are common. The impact this has on life opportunities, relationships and a person's emotional state is equally significant.

As we got closer to ending David B's art therapy, we also began to address the impact of having a diagnosis of Down's syndrome. He wrote some of his thoughts about this on large pieces of white paper, two of which are reproduced here:

Everybody needs friends. I find too hard in school (and) now at work to make friends. Sometimes I think I don't have any friends and who are they? Sometimes I go over the line saying he is my boyfriend. Sometimes I think nobody gives me respect and that upsets me. I think the main bit that no-one gives me respect is by having Down's syndrome. It is really got me down. Sometimes I say I don't have any friends because by having Down's syndrome. Why is it in my record because it make me feel bad and it hurts. Making friendships is not working because I feel very angry with having Down's syndrome.

This is the truth and nothing but the truth [about Down's syndrome]

It annoying .... true
I know I have not got it .... true
What is it doing in my records .... lie (someone else's)
Stops me making friendships .... true
Stops me being gay, makes me very very very very very very very very very very angry. I am still gay .... true
Why is everyone saying I got it? .... lie (that because they want to see [me] *upset)*
My family hate it .... true (never happened in my Dad's family)
Why did the test say positive not negative? .... lie (no test done)
My records was a mix up .... true
I have someone else's records say I got it .... true

This part of our work was extremely painful and the huge sense of injustice that David B felt became acutely apparent to me. However, it seemed as though this 'confrontation' with Down's syndrome also helped to bring about change and David B appeared determined that the diagnosis would not dominate his future.

The Beast

David B also used clay to create a piece that he named 'The Beast' (see Plate 9.2). This seemed to somehow combine his need for catharsis with his need to give form to the negative feelings he said he had felt burdened by for many years. The Beast was able to hold the intolerable feelings for David B in a concrete form and its construction seemed to liberate him. Through using the art materials, David B found his own way of containing and giving form to what had previously been chaotic and without form.

He says . . .

Well I had to get some of the steam out instead of me screaming the place down; I decided to build The Beast. Building The Beast is um making sure that I get every-thing out . . . instead of me letting off steam . . . so I decided to use the clay just to build The Beast . . . so I get all the tension out, get all the anxieties that I had deep down . . . so I had to bring that anxiety and um . . . I was expressing how I felt and um I had to build The Beast . . . so I get rid of all these inner feelings that I don't want to have . . . so I got the inner feelings out of me.

After The Beast was built, I felt relaxed and relieved and carrying on with life. By looking at The Beast after it's built, it's making me realise, the tension and the stress are out in the open. The Beast can scream instead of me doing it for The Beast.

A dream come true

When I went to meet with David B several years after therapy had finished, to dis-cuss writing this chapter, he told me he was planning to go to Gay Pride in Brighton the following month. This had been a dream of his for a long time and we decided to meet again soon after the event so that he could tell me about his experience there.

S: What was it like going to Gay Pride?

D: It was really exciting . . . everyone was very friendly . . . It was a really fun thing to do anyway; I've been waiting for that for a long time . . . even since I was a boy really.

S: So that was something that you've felt you wanted to be part of for many years?

D: Absolutely, yeah . . . absolutely . . . everybody was dressed up. I even noticed something in the crowd that caught my eye um . . . yeah that was . . . if you ever watch *Little Britain* . . . someone was just like Emily from *Little Britain*, oh they were fantastic.

S: It sounds very visual, lots of things to look at . . . colourful . . .

D: It was a very colourful day . . . I really enjoyed myself anyway . . . everybody dressed up . . . I was actually marching in the parade . . . that was fantastic . . .

S: So you were really part of this event?

D: Yep . . . I felt safer in the gay community . . . and it's just like what David Beckham said when he went to Real Madrid . . . he said 'It's a dream come true coming to Real Madrid', well me personally for going to Gay Pride . . . I say that's a dream come true . . . because I've been thinking about it for a long time . . . I really enjoyed it and I can't wait to do it again further down the line in the next few years.

I also bought a hat and a flag . . .

S: Your souvenirs of the day?

D: Yeah [getting out a pink cowboy hat and a large multicoloured flag] . . . This was what I got on Saturday. It was a really nice day out . . . it was a lovely day . . . so I took part really cos I felt part of the gay community for so long so I felt the need to join in really . . . Well it was the highlight of my year anyway and I'm glad I went . . . so fingers crossed, let's hope we'll organise this for next year.

When David B and I were talking about his experience of being part of Gay Pride, his whole face was alight with excitement and it was evident to me that this event had confirmed something really important for him about who he is.

Conclusion

When I first met David B, he surprised me and immediately challenged my own assumptions about people who have Down's syndrome. As I got to know him, he really got me thinking and inspired me. Image making that I thought began as an uncontrollable chaotic mess eventually became something with form that could contain all his internal contradictions within a healthy tension.

David B was clear that he needed to distance himself from the *persona* that he said had burdened him for so many years; his task in therapy was to find his authentic *self* and identity. He needed to be seen as an individual and not what others might assume a man with Down's syndrome should be. Through his own process of *individuation*, I felt that he found a truer sense of *self* and with this came the confidence to present himself as a man with many qualities, enabling others to begin to see his identity beyond his Down's syndrome.

References

Beart, S., Hardy, G. and Buchan, L. (2005). 'How People with Intellectual Disabilities View their Social Identity: A Review of the Literature'. *Journal of Applied Research in Intellectual Disabilities* 18(1): 47–56.

Hochheimer, W. (1969). *The Psychotherapy of C.G. Jung*. New York: C. G. Jung Foundation for Analytical Psychology Inc.

Jung, C. G. (1955). 'Psychology and Alchemy. Paragraph 44', in *Collected Works*. London: Routledge and Kegan Paul.

Jung, C. G. (1963). 'Mysterium Coniunctionis. Paragraph 616', in *Collected Works*. London: Routledge and Kegan Paul.

Von Franz, M. L. (1978). 'The Process of Individuation', in C. G. Jung (ed.) *Man and his Symbols*, pp. 157–254. London: Picador.

Talking about taking photographs

William

. . . one thing I really like doing . . . my hobby . . . photography . . . I want to be qualified . . . I want to be a qualified photographer . . . Taking photos . . . yeah . . .

. . . last time I took picture and got ball in mid-air . . . like one time I got a bird in mid-flight . . . got to act quickly . . . I very good taking photos. I know what I doing. I teach myself. I know about aperture – different apertures. I know about white balance. One thing I love taking . . . sunsets . . . sunsets . . . like aperture number 80 and sunset bring balance down and bring sunset up . . . sharpen it up. Learning and skill.

Yeah learning and skill and activity. One thing it very good. You've got to have a good eye . . . quick about it. You've got to know what you're doing.

So when you catch that ball in mid-air or that bird in mid-flight and look at it afterwards, how does it feel when you look at it?

Wow!

Conclusion

Kevin O'Farrell

This book began with the concept of something 'simple'. The emphasis was to produce a book that would be a good introduction to the landscape of learning disabilities as it is today and to provide insight into the role of art therapy within this. Our aim was to make it accessible to as wide an audience as possible whilst still being relevant to clinical practice. To this end we imagined a readership of trainees, new practitioners, carers, other professionals and those simply curious and wanting to understand this area of practice. Our focus was to highlight the most common themes for clinicians new to a landscape that can feel complex and overwhelming. For instance, we do not specifically explore autistic features or dual diagnosis (i.e., mental health and learning disability), which together with 750 known genetic causes for a learning disability can, perhaps, feel daunting for a new art therapist. However, we suggest that an understanding of the common themes is a baseline for successful therapy outcomes.

Reading the drafts and piecing together the various parts, we were struck by the wealth and diversity of material that has been woven together. Much of the richness is attributed to those with a learning disability, including the cover image. Aptly named 'windows', it captures the varied contributions made, and can be seen as one whole snapshot in time. It is, we feel, a book about people's lives and their feelings. 'When there are people who cannot think, remember, speak or write, it matters that others take up the scribe function' (Sinason 1992: 3). We believe that this book does that and, by working collaboratively, has directly elevated the voice of those who can speak but, arguably, have fewer opportunities to be heard.

In terms of this 'voice' we must be careful not to reduce our profession to that of 'champion of rights'. At a personal level we must search ourselves and ask, 'Why do we work here with this group of people and at this time?' Any underlying pain of difference, shame and injustice that has not found resolution in our lives as therapists (or paid workers) will be difficult to separate out from any therapeutic relationship. It is all too easy to get angry on behalf of someone else but this can blind us and ultimately prove very unhelpful for those we claim to be working for.

This is also a book that demonstrates a wide range of writing styles, drawing from the newly qualified to the experienced art therapist. Interviews and first person accounts have contributed to the tapestry. This has helped those for whom 'academia' has been a barrier to contribute to a book, and for their observations and experiences to be validated and prove useful to others.

This is not purely an academic book and we never intended it to be. Within therapy, thinking itself can be difficult enough without wading through literature that is creating further barriers to understanding. In learning disabilities we are already aware of one gap that is hard enough to bridge and have no wish to perpetuate another. However, with that thought in mind, we have provided a reading list at the end of this chapter which will further enrich understanding. It is by no means intended to be exclusive.

At the time of writing we are aware of a move within the therapies to an understanding of the basic ingredients in therapy that lead to successful outcomes, regardless of the orientation to which a particular therapy belongs. We welcome such discourses around attachment and mentalisation that, combined with research from neuroscience, help simplify what makes for progressive and successful interventions, and result in people's well-being.

Looking through this rich tapestry, I realise that, apart from Janet, there is a lack of the caregiver's voice, be that a parent, guardian, carer or support worker. This was in no way intentional but it highlights something very crucial. Within adult community teams there seems to be an element of treating the person as if they were an independent adult, a perspective influenced perhaps by 'normalisation'. Whilst full of good intention, it is a reality that for a significant number of adults with learning disabilities, their predominant relationships are formed with paid workers. It seems to me there is a real need to bridge a 'gap', where permissible, between the art room and life outside the art room. This can be difficult for the art therapist due to the confidential nature of the work. To some extent, this book has been written in an effort to bridge this gap and throughout the chapters there are examples of therapists who have innovatively stepped out of the classical art therapy role in order to be more effective.

There is a growing understanding and awareness that carers and support workers also need support. A recent study explored the role of perception and the training and support needs of staff. The conclusion was that support workers felt they needed 'a closer working relationship' with community teams 'to ensure implementation and maintenance of good practice' (Windley and Chapman 2010: 317). As art therapists we hope this book builds good foundations with caregivers and opens up the possibilities of working more closely.

So what about 'Don't guess my happiness!'? For me it's a well articulated and challenging statement that captures a number of intense frustrations. However, for Adam, the clearest grievance was that no one was seeing or accepting his unhappiness. For therapists this is part of the terrain, something that we expect as part of the process. Someone's unhappiness is not a reflection upon us, our work or character. When we delay the urge to make things better for someone we create a gap and an opportunity for the person we support to begin to think about their own solutions. Within this suspended space, imagination can be activated and the person can feel, with support, that they are learning and discovering something for themself. The biggest challenge, it seems, is how to develop this most basic listening space beyond the walls of therapy, where most relationships are of a paid *doing* rather than a *being* friendship quality. Within adult mental health it is well known that friendships are key to someone's recovery, but in learning disabilities to have someone who listens is very precious.

References

Sinason, V. (1992). *Mental Handicap and the Human Condition*. London: Free Association Books.

Windley, D. and Chapman, M. (2010). '"Support Workers" within Learning/Intellectual Disability Services: Perception of their Role, Training and Support Needs', *British Journal of Learning Disabilities* 38: 310–318.

Further reading

Books

De Groef, J. and Heinemann, E. (1999). *Psychoanalysis and Mental Handicap*. London: Free Association Books.

Rees, M. (ed.) (1998). *Drawing on Difference*. London: Routledge.

Sinason, V. (1992). *Mental Handicap and the Human Condition*. London: Free Association Books.

Oswin, M. (1991). *Am I Allowed to Cry? A Study of Bereavement Amongst People Who Have Learning Disabilities*. London: Souvenir Press (E&A) Ltd.

Journal articles

All references taken from *International Journal of Art Therapy: Inscape*

'Substance and Structure in the Art Therapeutic Process: Working with Mental Handicap', Anna Goldsmith, 1986, Issue 1.

'Transitional Phenomena and the Potential Space in Art Therapy with Mentally Handicapped People', Rose Hughes, 1988, Summer: 4–8.

'Challenging Assumptions: The Importance of Transference Processes in Work with People with Learning Difficulties', Robin Tipple, 1993, Summer: 2–9.

'Communication and Interpretation in Art Therapy with People Who Have a Learning Disability', Robin Tipple, 1994, Vol. 2: 31–35.

'Humpty Dumpty had a Great Fall', Margaret Stack, 1996, Vol. 2, No. 1: 1–13.

'Just Forging, or Seeking Love and Approval? An Investigation into the Phenomenon of the Forged Art Object and the Copied Picture in Art Therapy Involving People with Learning Disabilities', Barrie Damarell, 1999, Vol. 4, No. 2: 44–50.

'Working with Sex Offenders who have a Learning Disability', Karen McKenzie, Duncan Chisholm and George Murray, 2000, Vol. 5, No. 2.

'The Interpretation of Children's Artwork in a Paediatric Disability Setting', Robin Tipple, 2003, Vol. 8, No. 2: 48–59.

'Examination of the Changes that Take Place During an Art Therapy Intervention', Hillary

Pounsett, Karen Parker, Alison Hawtin and Suzanne Collins, 2006, Vol. 11, No. 2: 79–101.

'Wrapping Things Up: Ending Art Therapy with Two Adults with Learning Disabilties', Stephanie Bull, 2008, Vol. 13, No. 2: 74–78.

Other journals

'Isobel's Images: One Woman's Experience of Art Therapy', Isobel White, Stephanie Bull and Mary Beavis, 2008, *British Journal of Learning Disabilties* 37: 103–109.

'Counteracting Isolation: Group Art Therapy for People with Learning Difficulties', Sue Strand, 1990, *Group Analysis* 23: 255–263.

Index

An environmentally friendly book printed and bound in England by www.printondemand-worldwide.com

This book is made entirely of sustainable materials; FSC paper for the cover and PEFC paper for the text pages.

#0263 - 160715 - C8 - 234/156/11 - PB - 9780415583244